GOSHEN, NEW YORK

GOSHEN,
NEW YORK

HISTORY,
THE FABRIC OF A TOWN

SANDRA ROTHENBERGER

Epigraph Books
Rhinebeck, New York

Goshen, New York: History, the Fabric of a Town © Copyright 2025 by
Sandra Rothenberger

Paperback ISBN 9781966293200

Library of Congress Control Number 2025920445

Book and cover design by Colin Rolfe

Epigraph Books
22 East Market Street, Suite 304
Rhinebeck, New York 12572
(845) 876-4861
epigraphpublishing.com

Introduction

The word "fabric" in the title of this book does not represent cloth but structure, framework, construction, and foundation. These are the defining qualities that a town is built upon.

There are nine short stories that are not strictly history in the sense of the word, but the events that occurred to designate it as historic. Three of the short stories are my individual experiences: Case Cemetery, Haunted Farmhouse and Mystery at Viking Hill Farm.

Dutchess Quarry Caves is an important archeological site pertaining to the first inhabitants of Goshen from the Ice Age, 12,500 years ago. Will the town of Goshen save Dutchess Quarry Caves? Residents in Goshen and surrounding towns are waiting for a decision from the Orange County Executive and Goshen Town Board to decide on how they will manage this situation.

Presently, Goshen has 32 historical markers throughout the town. Occasionally a new marker will be added. A marker contains a summary about people, places and events that occurred at that location. I have selected fifteen of those markers to tell the whole story.

To my daughter Amanda Schiffmacher who made growing up fun.

About the Front Cover

Goshen Territory

Wawayanda Patent

European settlement plans for Goshen were made in 1654. A large land grant known as the Wawayanda Patent of 150,000 acres was granted in 1703, by the colonial government, to John Bridges and eleven of his associates. The land grant was approved by Queen Anne of England that contained two laws.

Extinguishment of Indian Rights: Before the formal grant in 1703, the rights of the twelve Indian Chiefs living on the land were extinguished in transaction with them.

Boundaries: The original grant defined the patent's boundaries. The Highlands of the Hudson on the east, the Orange-Ulster County line on the north, and the New York-New Jersey boundary on the South.

Sarah Wells

Christopher Denne and eleven of his associates held the Wawayanda patent on 150,000 acres of land in Goshen. The stipulation for ownership of the land was one of the twelve men had to live on the land by a certain date.

Sarah Wells, a 16-year-old indentured servant, lived with Christopher Denne and Madam Elizabeth Denne of New York City. Christopher Denne traveled to Goshen to survey his land and returned to New York. In 1712 Christopher Deene sent Sara to the unsettled frontier of Goshen to fulfill the requirements of the patent. Christopher Deene promised Sarah 100 acres of land if she established a homestead. Sarah with three carpenters and three native Munsee Indians as guides, sailed across the Hudson River in a single mast sloop, landing at Plum Point in New Windsor. Their destination was the Moodna Creek in Cornwall six miles away.

They traveled by canoe up the Moodna Creek, Otterkill Creek, and through a swamp to arrive at the uncivilized land of Goshen. Sarah was the first European to settle in Goshen. Her travels required her to confront unknown wilderness, water infested by snakes, Native Americans, and beasts of prey.

When arriving at her destination, a small family group of Munsee Indians built her a wigwam by the Otterkill Creek, taught her party how to protect themselves and plant crops.

In 1718, Sarah married William Bull, a stonemason from Wolverhampton, Staffordshire, England. She kept her given name, Wells. The swamp the group traveled through to reach Goshen was named by William's father, Peter Bull, from a source only known by him: Purgatory Swamp.

Sarah Wells' revolutionary efforts established the town of Goshen. Her extraordinary bravery was recognized by naming a major road on the outskirts of Goshen after her: Sarah Wells Trail.

Goshen
"The Land of Plenty and Blessings"
Biblical Meaning: Utopian Quality

The Town of Goshen was organized by an act on March 7, 1788. In the East, the land was hilly, in the West flat and marshy. The Drowned Lands of soil loam contained slate and limestone. The Otterkill creek and a branch of Murderer's Kill Creek crossed the land. The Village of Goshen was founded in 1722, and incorporated March 28, 1809.

Contents

David Henry Haight

NAPKNOLL ESTATE

1836 – 1901

Haight Mansion
Goshen Public Library and Historical Society

Standing prominently on the outskirts of Goshen was a Greek Revival structure, dated 1836, known as the David Henry Haight Mansion. The mansion survived 150 years before it was torn down. Today only a few remnants of various buildings remain. Visible from main street are the stone foundation of the house, a 30-foot tall stone chimney used to heat two greenhouses, a restored caretakers house, and a large granite Haight family mausoleum.

David Henry Haight and Mary Ellen Jansen Haight
Goshen Public Library and Historical Society

HAIGHT GENEAOLOGY

The Haight name is spelled in several ways depending on the clan they belonged to in Europe. The Haight name was spelled Hoyt, Hoit, Hayts, Haite, and Hought.

Simon Hoyte (1590-1657) of West Hatch, Somerset England, married Jane Stoodlie (1596-1628) of Marshwood Dorset, England in 1617. They had three sons: Walter Hoyte (1618-1699), Nicholas Hoyte (1620-1655), and John Hoyte (1628-1684). Simon, with his wife and three sons, sailed across the Atlantic on the ship Lyons Whelp, arriving in Salem, Massachusetts April 26, 1628. The spelling of their last name Hoyt was recorded as Haight when they arrived in Massachusetts. They settled in Dorchester, Massachusetts, then moved to Windsor, Connecticut in 1640. The Haight family name was established in America.

Nicholas Haight (1620-1655), married Susanna Joyce (1626-1655) on July 12, 1646. They had four children: Samuel (1647-1712), Jonathan (1649-1696), David (1651-1704) and Daniel (1653-1655).

Samuel Haight (1647-1712), married Sarah Noble (1651-1712).

The Haight family increased in size, and they migrated South to New York City.

Jacob Haight (1705-1767), married Sarah Hicks (1710-1767) November 6, 1733, in Queens, New York. A son was born to them, **John**. They lived in Oswego, Dutchess County, New York.

John Haight (1738-1809), the patriarch of the Haight family in New York, married Abigail Haviland (1738-1831) in 1759. They had 11 children. One of their sons, **David Lane** was born in Rye, Westchester County, New York.

David Lane Haight (1755-1851), married Ann Kip (1778-1855), and they had four children: Richard Kip (1798-1864), Ann Matilde (1801-1870), **David Henry** (1805-1872), and Abigail Jane 1807-1888).

David Henry Haight married Mary Ellen Jansen in 1836, and they resided on an estate known as Napknoll in Goshen, New York.

Note: In the seventeenth and eighteenth centuries, male children would be given the first name of the father. The only distinction between father and son would be a middle name. The name David Henry Haight followed this tradition.

ACQUIRING THE LAND

In the 1700 and 1800 hundreds when a landowner died, the deed would transfer his property to his children. Ownership changed many times, but the land stayed in the family for hundreds of years. Dr. Samuel Gale, the father of Benjamin Gale (1734-1805) and his wife Eleanor Carpenter (d.1787) owned 183 acres in Goshen. In his will, Benjamin Gale left his property to Anthony Carpenter (1715-1790), a relative of his wife Elenor. Anthony Carpenter was one of the executors of the will of Benjamin Gale dated 28 Feb.1782. The will was proved 22 Mar. 1786. Anthony deeded the property to his son James.

In 1817 James Carpenter deeded his property to his three children in equal parts, Fannie (Frances) Jansen, James W. Carpenter, and Mary Johnson. Fannie Jansen became the sole owner of the 183 acres after the death of her brother, James W. Carpenter, and sister Mary Johnson.

In 1834 Fannie Jansen left the property equally to her five children, John J., Dewitt D., John, Nathan R., and Mary Ellen.

The Jansen lineage can be traced back to 1719 to William Bull and Sarah Wells.

In 1836 Mary Ellen Jansen married David Henry Haight, and they started the lengthy process of buying the land from Mary Ellen's siblings.

1844 purchased the property of John J. and his wife Mary (Heard)

1846 purchased the property of Dewitt D. and his wife Mary Ann (Duryea)

1857 purchased the property of John and Elizabeth Wallace

1864 purchased the property of Nathan R. and Caroline Johnson

It took David Henry and Mary Ellen 20 years to restore the property to the original 183 acres. This property stayed intact for 164 years by passing the property to their children.

INTRODUCTION

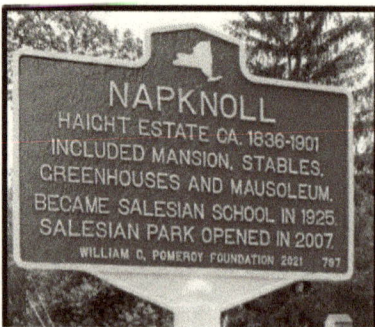

255 Main Street

The Haight's were astute business people opening several shops in New York, offering wares that were needed by the people. As the needs of the people changed, so did the offerings of their businesses. All their shops were remarkably successful making the Haight family wealthy. They were accepted in the aristocratic circles of high society of New York City.

David met Mary Ellen Jansen in Manhattan in the late 1820's. They would marry and live on an estate in Goshen known as Napknoll.

THE RISE OF A MANSION

After David Henry and Mary Ellen married, they commenced in developing her property of 183 acres, in Goshen, New York, into an estate of grandeur. It was the Greek Revival Style, and wealthy people spared no expense in building their large houses with extraordinary elegance and architectural detail.

David was a decedent of the French-Huguenots and had strong religious convictions. His belief was Episcopalian, and because of his beliefs, placement of the mansion became a topic of discussion of the townspeople. The direction in which a church or building faced, followed ancient tradition and Christian symbolism. Instead of building the house with the front facing Main Street, it was turned to face the same direction as the 1812 Presbyterian Church. The front of the house and the Presbyterian Church both faced Church Street.

Developing the property into an estate began in 1836. The mansion was built incorporating Mary Ellens house and property. The Greek Revival style house with Corinthian columns would be 7,800 square feet. Field stones and bricks were used to build the foundation measuring 82 feet by 96 feet. The structure was wood frame with many architectural details.

The main entrance of the house had a porte-cochere (a coach porch), so arriving guests could depart from their carriages away from the inclement weather. The road from the coach porch ended in a courtyard where the carriages would wait for their occupants. The raised porch had two sets of slate steps. The main door was a four-panel painted wood door, flanked by side lights of leaded glass, and a glass elliptical fanlight over the door.

The roof was made of grey slate with 7 gabled dormer attic

windows. One end of the house had a gambrel (4 sided) roof. The four-round arched red brick chimneys, one double, displayed a keystone made of carved white marble. Ornamentation of metal stars were placed on each chimney.

Windows were plentiful giving the interior excellent light. (A lite is 1 piece of window glass.) The first floor had 12-lite French windows, the southern porch had 3 pairs of 8-lite casement windows. The upstairs attic windows were ample with round arched sashes, 6-lite over one large windowpane.

The west end of the house had a distinctive double-storied pentagonal bay window. Pentagonal bay windows were in favor in the town, and many houses displayed the same design throughout Goshen. Their shape represented the six days of creation.

Entering the main door there were three steps that terminated at the main central staircase. The hallway from the foyer continued to the back of the house. A small staircase at the back of the house rose from the kitchen to the attic. The staff used the back stairs.

The first floor had eight rooms. There were three salons that were used for entertaining. A salon could be a drawing room, a reception room, or a music room. These rooms were social meeting places where the hostess set the agenda. The first floor was completed with a library, a large oval dining room and two enclosed porches, one at each end of the house.

The ceilings were 10 feet high with five-foot-high paneling topped by large ornate crown moldings. The main floor was heated by five fireplaces, four of them with classical stone surrounds. The library had a magnificent fireplace with dark stained oak. The remainder of the room was carved oak woodwork, oak bookcases, and gas lighting.

The most magnificent room on this level was the oval dining room with nine-foot paneled walls that were topped with large crown moldings. There was a built-in serving buffet, dumbwaiter, and two lead-glass cabinets. The fireplace was the showcase of the room. It was 10 feet high and had an opening 10 feet wide. The mantel was so large and heavy that it had to be supported by two marble columns.

The kitchen was the area where the staff stayed during the day.

The meals prepared in the kitchen were sent to the dining room by a dumbwaiter to be served by the dining room staff.

The second floor had nine bedrooms and four baths with four additional fireplaces. Houses were heated by fireplaces until the late 1800's.

The third floor had an additional eight bedrooms, three baths, and no fireplaces. At the top of the third-floor staircase, a 10x10 stained glass skylight was built into the ceiling. Attic bedrooms in mansions were reserved for the servants.

David Henry and Mary Ellen had five children: Fannie, Henry, Edward, Charles, and Egbert. Three of the Haight's children died. Fannie died at the age of two, Charles died on the island of Cuba from yellow fever at the age of 28, and Egbert died at the age of 19. Henry resided on the property and Edward lived in New York City.

David Henry and Mary Ellen had the opportunity to purchase additional property. Combining the 183 acres with the purchase of additional land, resulted in an estate of 400 acres. Today that property line would be Main Street, Sarah Wells Trail, Coleman Road, Old Chester Road and South Church Street. It included the Slate Hill Cemetery. Sarah Wells Trail and Coleman Road were previously known as Newburgh Road.

HAIGHT MAUSOLEUM

In 1872 four and one-half acres were set aside for a large family mausoleum. The architectural style was Dutch, the stone was granite, and cost $75,000 thousand dollars to build. Today that would be $1.8 million dollars. Inside, the floors are marble, the crypts are lined with copper, and the double door entrance gate is bronze. There is also a small chapel inside.

To the side of the mausoleum is a 1875 Dutch style brick caretaker's cottage. It was orginally landscaped with an English Knot Garden. The cottage has been maintained and the outside is in good condition. The downstairs has been restored; the upstairs is in the original condition.

Haight Mausoleum

Caretaker's Cottage

LANDSCAPING THE ESTATE

David was a multi-millionaire and spared no expense in landscaping Napknoll. His choices of specimens for landscaping were not confined just to American species but were imported from Europe as well. His travels through Europe influenced his vision in developing his property. It would be a grandiose setting on par with the elegance of New York City.

David wanted the property to be a grand summer home where he could return after traveling to New York City. He laid out a park with drives and walks, constructed an artificial lake and made it a showcase in the area. Flower gardens and orchards were added among the lush lawns in addition to ponds and grazing lands.

Gazebo
Goshen Public Library and Historical Society

Over one hundred tall, beautiful pine trees were imported from Europe to line the driveway and walks around the property. Other trees and shrubs were also imported from Europe. In a severe wind-storm in the early 1900's many of the trees were blown down.

The property was enclosed with wrought iron fencing with five openings, two for carriages and three for foot traffic. A foot gate, at the side of the property, was accessed from Main Street. It was semicircu-lar in design with four granite pillars. The wrought iron fence displayed several H's for Haight. The front walk was made of slate slabs.

Front Gate
255 Main Street

View of Landscaped Property
Goshen Public Library and Historical Society

David imported sheep and cattle from Europe to graze among the property. Farm buildings were added to store carriages, equip-ment to maintain the property, and a barn for cattle and sheep.

Mr. & Mrs. Haight in carriage by the farm buildings
Goshen Public Library and Historical Society

Haight Greenhouse
Goshen Public Library and Historical Society

David's travels throughout Europe influenced the design of his fountains. Several fountains could be found throughout the property. The most magnificent one was near the front gate and could be viewed by travelers on Main Street. A small artistic pool with a fountain was by the house.

Several fountains inside the greenhouses presented an atmosphere of tranquility. Two greenhouses were constructed that produced fruit and flowers year around. The greenhouses were heated by a 30-foot-tall stone chimney that today stands next to the Goshen Public Library and Historical Society.

After graduating from St. Paul's College at Concord, David's grandson, David L., became involved in the greenhouses and started a business of raising flowers. He built eight additional large greenhouses on the estate grounds, encompassing several acres. His specialty was propagating roses, palms, and violets. John Logan was his greenhouse manager, and due to his solid judgment and intelligence regarding flowers, the products from the greenhouses were popular and in demand.

David was the first American to import the Scottish Belted Galloway cattle from Holland to the United States. In 1838, the U.S. Consul of Holland arranged the importation of cattle to D. H. Haight of Goshen, New York. The second importation of this unusual breed was in 1848 by P.T. Barnum, circus showman, who also had a farm of these cattle in Orange County, New York.

Scottish Belted Galloway Cattle

Also called Dutch Belted cattle they are known as the Lakenvelder, a term meaning a blanket around the body. They resemble an Oreo cookie. They are a high producer of rich milk. David's grandson David L. continued to raise the breed at the Heard Farm on the property in Goshen. His large herd of dairy cows became a profitable business

NEW YORK CITY, NEW YORK

The Haight family has a long history in New York City dating back to 1738 when the patriarch, John Haight was born. They were shrewd

12

businesspeople, always looking towards the future and anticipating new adventures in business. The Haight's became a family of wealthy successful merchants and landowners who socialized with the upper class of the city. They were educated, sometimes in European universities. They traveled to other parts of the world to establish their businesses.

New York City was home to the most millionaires in America. John D. Rockefeller owned Standard Oil Company, Andrew Carnegie made his fortune in railroads and owned one of the largest steel manufacturing companies in the world, Cornelius Vanderbilt owned the steamship industry and John Jacob Astor owned a large amount of real estate in New York City.

David Henry was the youngest of four children with two sisters, and one brother. All the Haight children married into prominent families.

Abigail married General Mallet, and they resided at the U.S. consul in Florence, Italy.

Ann Matilde married David Piffard, whose father was a celebrated banker of London. In 1824, he and his wife moved to a hamlet in Livingston, New York. His reputation proceeded him and the hamlet where they lived was named Piffard. There were 150 residents, one church, one store, a post office, one hotel, a blacksmith and wagon shop, a sawmill, and a barrel factory. David built his estate, Westerly, now a historic home added to the National Register of Historic Places.

David Piffard, Westerly Estate

Richard Kipp married Sarah Rogers on December 12, 1826. Richard died November 2, 1862, of congestion of the lungs and diseases of the brain. He is buried at New York Marble Cemetery, Manhattan, in vault 147 of David L. Haight.

David Henry's ambitions made him a wealthy businessman in New York. His success started at D.L. & J.E. Haight & Co. working for his father in the family's businesses. He invested in real estate, established many businesses, and owned two hotels. He was Director at the St. Nicholas Bank and the Manhattan Life Insurance Company.

The American Industrial Revolution started in New York in 1817 with the opening of the Erie Canal. It was a time of fast paced living with numerous inventions and a booming economy. Life was becoming a period of convenience that mimicked the British style of living. Many businesspeople became millionaires and one of those men was David Henry Haight.

David L. Haight started a business of saddlery and leather goods located at 195 Broadway. Horse drawn carriages, delivery wagons, and any horse drawn conveyance of transportation of that era needed harnesses, saddles, and other leather items. Their reputation for fine leather goods was so successful they had to upgrade to a larger building.

David L. Height. anticipated the future needs of the people and opened a dry goods store. These stores became a social gathering place for the ladies. It was a new concept that numerous items could be purchased at the same location versus individual stores.

David Henry worked for his father in the dry goods store for three years as a clerk before joining the business as a partner in 1827. He was 22 years old. The house of D. L. & J. E. Haight & Co. was one of the most prosperous in New York City.

The United States continued to grow, and this growth resulted in hostilities around the world. In Europe, war between France and Great Britain resulted in the United States declaring war on Great Britain in 1812. This was the "The Second American Revolution." An embargo of goods from Great Britian caused the dry good stores to fail. D.L. & J. E. Haight & Co. was one of them.

The war with the British ended in 1814 and in 1816 the house of D. L. Haight engaged in a new wholesale jobbing business. He opened a business that used leather strips called skivers used in book-binding, to trim hats, shoes, and other clothing. The business sold 20,000 dozen skivers a year. It was a very profitable business; several branches were established in other countries.

In 1835, David Sr. located the primary business from 165 Pearl Street to 170 Water Street. The old store was razed, and on the grounds, David Sr. built the second hotel in New York City, the Franklin House Hotel at 164 E. 87th Street. The first hotel in New York was the City Hotel on Broadway between Thames and Cedar Streets.

The Franklin House was a prestigious Egyptian style building located in Manhattan a short distance from Madison Avenue. It had 9 floors, rooms decorated with fine artwork, exceptional service, and a large staff. The breakfast lounge and restaurant offered French cuisine. It overwhelmed the City Hotel in terms of size, amenities, and services.

In 1835 David Sr. moved his residence to No. 15 Waverly Place and David Henry moved his residence next door to No. 13 Waverly Place. The Haight's resided in their luxurious homes in New York City during the winter months. In the summer months, David Henry would travel to his summer houses located in Goshen, New York and Bar Harbor, Maine.

David's ambitions for architecture resulted in several exceptional buildings he built throughout his lifetime. In his early years he invested in real estate in New York City, built the Insurance Buildings at 156-158 Broadway and his large house on Madison Avenue. He inherited the Franklin House Hotel from his father, built the famous St. Nicholas Hotel, and restored the Hotel Lambat in Paris, France, saving it from collapse.

The opulent St. Nicholas Hotel, the finest hotel in the United States, was located on the west side of Broadway between Spring and Broome Streets. The 6-story 350 room hotel was a pure white marble building of Italian architecture with Corinthian elements. The entrance was a pure white marble lobby, frescoed ceilings, and gilded domed skylights adorned every ceiling. It accommodated 1,000 guests a week, had several dining rooms, a reading room, a gentlemen's hair salon and a drawing room.

The Lost 1853 St. Nicholas Hotel -- Broadway between Broome and Spring

ST. NICHOLAS HOTEL, BROADWAY, NEW YORK.
TREADWELL, ACKER & CO., PROPRIETORS.

Print from Frank Leslie's Illustrated Monthly,
New York Public Library Collection

It opened for business on January 6, 1853. This was the year the World Exposition at the Crystal Palace in New York opened. With its lavish appointments, it was the hotel of choice for those attending the Exposition.

It was the first hotel in New York City to cost $1 million dollars to build and $7 hundred thousand to furnish. In one year, its popularity resulted in an expansion to 900 rooms that encompassed the entire block. The St. Nicholas was the hotel of choice over the Astor Hotel built by John Jacob Astor.

Hotels in this era were used as second homes. High society clientele would come to New York to enjoy an extended vacation to experience the culture, theater, and museums in the city. It was not unusual for families to stay for several weeks.

The luxury of the St. Nicholas hotel was not to be surpassed by any other hotel establishment. The first floor displayed a white oak staircase illuminated by a gas chandelier costing $1,100. The second-floor dining room had rosewood furniture with satin damask upholstery and could accommodate 400 guests. The rosewood piano had pearl keys instead of ivory. The numerous chandeliers in the dining area contained 20 gas lights each. The silverware was Sheffield plate.

Many rooms had marble mantle fireplaces although the hotel had central heating provided by three iron steam boilers in the basement. The steam boilers also powered a washer-drier machine capable of doing 5,000 pieces of laundry a day. Each room had hot and cold running water, gas, and a water closet. Rooms had an intercom system directly to the front desk to request service. It was the first hotel to have a bridal chamber decorated entirely in satin.

Society found the hotel a respite from the pressures of the time. There were two balls every week for New Yorkers to dance the night away. There was a caveat. The hotel had a bar room. Only European establishments had bar rooms and David Henry was influenced by European culture to put one in the St. Nicholas.

In September 1855, the patrons became indignant when Captain J. J. Wright and his partner R. S. Dean from the steamship, Jewess, had a loud verbal argument. It became violent when Captain Wright pulled out a cowhide strap from his pocket and struck Dean across the face. Instantly, Dean drew a large bowie knife from under his vest and plunged it deeply into the side of Wright. Dean attempted to flee when Wright plunged the knife into Dean's abdomen mortally wounding him.

In 1861 the hotel hosted a grand ball to celebrate Jackson's victory in the Battle of New Orleans. Generals, Majors, Colonels, Commodore's, and New York's high society danced into the early hours of the morning. The hotel was home to many celebrities including Lavinia Warren who married General Tom Thumb in the Grace Church.

The Civil War would not end until 1865. In 1864 a group of Confederate conspirators devised a plan to burn down New York City. The group's plan was to stay in various hotels across the city and synchronize their efforts to set them on fire. On the evening of November 25 at 8:40 p.m., it was discovered that the St. Nicholas was on fire. By morning, there were eleven hotels on fire. The hotel staff, patrons and firefighters worked through the night to extinguish the fires and the plan to burn down New York City was thwarted. The repairs on the St. Nicholas hotel were completed fourteen years later, in 1878.

By the 1870's, people wanted to be in uptown New York, and the Fifth Avenue Hotel on Broadway was their choice. Uptown offered many museums, theaters, dining establishments and stores where most tourists wanted to be, near the entertainment district.

On March 4, 1884, the St. Nicholas Hotel announced it would be closing. The furnishings were auctioned off on March 31, 1884, at incredibly low prices.

Demolition of the white marble St. Nicholas Hotel started on May 1. One of the most prestigious elegant hotels in the world was gone. Someone had the foresight to preserve two sections of the hotel that are now apartments at 521 and 523 Broadway. The white marble façade was preserved on the apartments and is known to be the finest white marble façade in New York City.

LIFE IN THE 1800'S

The pace of living in the 1800's was slow and deliberate. Existence depended on knowing where to obtain daily needs for themselves, operation of the estate, their farmland, and animals. The staff and workers managed these chores.

The Haight's access to New York City afforded them to purchase their finer items, such as clothing and shoes, in Manhattan. Wardrobes were small, especially for women, as styles changed every ten years. Men had their haberdashery shops were a tailor custom made his suits and women had their dressmaker where a seamstress sewed her clothing. Material for women's clothing was imported from Paris such as silks, damasks, and brocades.

Meals were a special occasion. Breakfast was considered the second largest meal attended by the entire family. The largest meal of the day was served between 1 p.m. and 3 p.m. and was a hot meal. Afternoon tea was served around 4 p.m. attended only by women. Supper or high tea was served at 6 p.m. and attended by the whole family. Until 1875, meals were prepared on open hearths, coal, or wood stoves.

Fish was a main staple at all the meals. Living close to the Hudson River, oysters were plentiful as well as other types of fish. They also enjoyed eels, turtles, and squirrels.

The Haight's had their dairy cattle at the Heard Farm to supply them with fresh dairy products of milk, cream, and butter. The farmland produced vegetables, potatoes, and legumes. Chickens and ducks supplied eggs. The heated greenhouses supplied fruit, herbs, and flowers throughout the year. Fruit was also imported: oranges from Sicily, bananas from Cuba, and pumpkins from Chile. Only the wealthy could afford imported fruit.

Cocktails were served at mealtimes. In 1803 a cocktail would consist of sugar, water, and bitters. In 1823 bourbon became available, 1831 whiskey would be offered, and 1850 gin was added to the selection. Wine was introduced in the 1840's and was a sweet drink. After the American Civil War of 1861-1865, beer was offered to the public. Only men drank beer.

Formal dinners were held in private homes for family and friends although Goshen was fortunate to have two operating inns. The 1747 Stagecoach Inn and the 1790 Orange Inn.

Traveling from one point to another was arduous. Local travel was by carriage on dirt roads. Going to Europe was by steam powered ocean liner.

Goshen's first post office opened after the Revolutionary war of 1775-1783. Writing letters was the only communication over long distances. The mail was not dependable since it could take days for a letter to travel from New York City to Goshen. It was common for mail to be carried by family or friends traveling between Goshen and Manhattan.

A letter sent from New York City post office traveled by steamship ferry across the Hudson River to Newburgh where the Erie railroad would transport it to Goshen. It would be delivered by the Goshen post office. Delivery of the mail to Goshen residents, was by men dressed in black wool suits.

Letters were about everyday life, family, friends, church, and town events. The upper class could afford to buy writing paper which they shared with family and friends.

The following are excerpts from letters written between Fannie Jansen of Goshen and her daughter Mary Ellen Jansen living in New York City. The letters are dated 1828-1834 before Mary Ellen married David Henry Height.

Dear Daughter

I did not receive your letter till Saturday evening; the mail was miscarried and came by Newburgh. I began to be quite uneasy. We hear so much of the scarlet fever in N.Y. If I do not hear often I cannot but feel all a mother's fears for the welfare of her only child

My dear Daughter

I do not hear much about your going to church and whether any of you attend the evening meetings. I am afraid you are all too much taken up with the world and neglect the one thing that is needful. Your mother is rejoicing that the Lord has not forsaken his church here. It is but little better than a week ago but very few attended prayer meetings. Last Wednesday was the first full meeting, it was at Daniel Wells then the houses have been filled to overflowing twice this week.

Envelope Address: Miss Mary Ellen Jansen
To the care of Ms. Jeromus Johnson   New York

Mr. Wilsons child little Helen is dead. They were waiting for him at

Newburgh. He rode home that night; she is to be buried today—give my love to all in great haste your Papa is waiting for the letter. Your affectionate mother F

A number of these letters were purchased and are at the Goshen Public Library and Historical Society. Goshen's Historian Michelle Figliomeni evaluated the letters for the library collection.

David and Mary Ellen's family were held in high esteem in the town of Goshen. The Haight's participated in the life of Goshen and were considered as kind and generous people. They employed many of the towns' people on the estate.

Relating the following story was disturbing about the integrity of the Height family. It was created by community gossip and misjudgment by the police.

Father Kennedy, an Episcopal priest residing in Cuba, was a good friend of the Haights. One day he witnessed a woman who was abusing a young boy by whipping his face and head with a belt buckle resulting in severe injuries. He removed the boy from the woman's care and obtained permission from the United States consulate to bring the boy to the United States. He knew the generosity of the Haight's, and when he asked them to take the boy until he could return from Cuba, they readily agreed.

In Philadelphia, Mr. Joseph Ross reported to the police that his son, Charley Ross, had been abducted. Sheriff James W. Hoyt of Goshen received a Pinkerton Agency flyer about Charley Ross's abduction and a photo of the boy.

Gossip about the abduction in Philadelphia spread around Goshen very quickly. Many residents reported to the police that a boy answering the description of the abducted boy had been mysteriously secluded for several days at the mansion of David Henry Haight. They even concocted the story that they had spoken to the boy who told them that his name was Charley, and he had been transported from Philadelphia in a wagon.

Sheriff Hoyt, believing the gossip of the townspeople, went to the estate. David was not home because he spent six months in

Manhattan doing business. Mrs. Haight received him and explained to Sheriff Hoyt the story of Father Kennedy bringing the boy from Cuba to be kept in her care until he returned. Mrs. Haight did not present the boy saying he was sleeping and recovering from his injuries. Sheriff Hoyt did not believe her.

Sheriff Hoyt went back to his office and retrieved the Pinkerton flyer with the boy's picture and returned to the estate. Mrs. Haight was deeply offended that her word was not credible. With much conversation, Sheriff Hoyt convinced excited Mrs. Haight to let him see the boy.

Sheriff Hoyt compared the Pinkerton photo to the boy. He determined that it was Charley Ross because of a cowlick on the left side of his forehead, noticeably light eyebrows, and brown eyes. Sheriff Hoyt went back to his office and Mrs. Haight hired a lawyer.

Sheriff Hoyt sent a telegram to the Philadelphia police. "There is a child here which I believe is the lost Charley Ross." Charley's father, Joseph, agreed to make the trip to Goshen to identify his son. Upon seeing the boy, he determined it was not his son. Joseph Ross presented a certificate to Mrs. Haight sparing her from further annoyance.

Sheriff Hoyt believed in the gossip of the townspeople. He offended one of most prestigious families in Goshen.

DOWNFALL OF A MANSION

David Henry Haight passed away Saturday, April 29, 1876, in New York City at the age of 71. He had been ill nine weeks prior to his passing. The funeral was in New York City and the following Tuesday morning his ashes would be taken to Goshen to be placed in the Haight family mausoleum that afternoon.

A group of family and friends accompanied the casket transported from New York City to Goshen. The group traveled by steamboat across the Hudson River to Newburgh. They boarded the Erie Train which had a direct line to the center of Goshen. Parlor cars were reserved for the group to freshen up, rest and receive refreshments. Goshen was in mourning.

The Supreme Court referee Peter B. Olaney received David's will and recommended that the Haight landmarks be sold in New York City. These included the St. Nicholas building on Broadway, near Spring Street, the Haight buildings at 156-158 Broadway near Liberty Street, and the Jansen buildings at 13 and 15 Waverly Place. All these buildings were in the downtown section of Manhattan.

Before David's death, he put the Goshen property into a trust and willed it to his wife, Mary Ellen Jansen Haight. After David's passing, Mary Ellen became overwhelmed running Napknoll estate. She moved to her New York residence at 284 Madison Avenue and enlisted her grandson, David L. Haight, to help manage the property according to the trust.

After David's death, Mary Ellen wrote her will, in accordance with the trust, with the following provisions…

"Having by my will give my trustees power to sell any of the real estate devised by them in trust and to sell the Heard Farm at Goshen, Orange County."

"I further authorize them to sell any other part or parts of my real estate…provided, however, that no part of my estate devised to either of my sons for life shall be sold during the lifetime of the son to whom the same is so devised, except with his consent."

"In case of a sale of any part or parts of my estate before the time shall arrive for a final division of the part or parts so sold, I authorize my said trustees to invest and keep invested the proceeds thereof…"

Mary Ellen Haight died February 19, 1895. She was interred at the family mausoleum at Napknoll. Her will appointed Stephen D. Hatch and Thomas L. Ogden as trustees and executors of her will with instructions to replace vacancies. The trustees would inherit the estate upon Mary Ellen's death and would be managed according to her will. Unfortunately, both Hatch and Ogden died before the will was recorded.

Mary Ellen wanted to keep her fortune intact during the lifetime of her sons and their wives and to transmit the same to her grandchildren, but she was reluctant to permit the title to vest in her own sons. She did not want the estate to be retained as real estate to be sold, but instead in trust. The will stated that proceeds from bonds, real estate, and securities of New York State should be used to keep the estate intact. The courts would not honor her will since it had not been filed.

The sons, Edward C. and Henry J. Haight brought proceedings in Westchester County sometime around October 24, 1896, for the courts to honor their mothers' will as written. Their request was denied.

After the deaths of Hatch and Ogden, John K. Myers, and Francis W. Nuboer were appointed by the courts as trustees to administer her trust and will. They determined they had the same power as Hatch and Ogden, but the property would be sold.

They blatantly ignored Mary Ellen's will regarding how the estate was to be managed after her death. She had wanted the property to stay in trust and be passed down to her two sons, their wives, and her grandchildren.

The dishonest appointed trustees of the courts committed a crime by not honoring the will although it was not recorded. They failed to acknowledge the reputation of the Haight family. They sold the property. They stole the estate from its heirs.

The court's order to sell the property was issued on February 2, 1901. David Henry Haight's efforts were a lynchpin of Goshen's growth.

These tragic events led to the downfall of the Haight property known as Napknoll estate.

The property was known as Haight's Park until 1991. The last owner of the property, a Roman Catholic brotherhood known as Salesian sold the property in 1991. Many were referring to the property as Salesian Park. The town lawyer said officials should stop referring to it as Salesian to avoid legal problems. The town officials held a vote asking the residents for suggestions to rename the park. It was named Salesian Park to the dismay of many residents. The boys that attended the Salesian St. Michaels school were haunted by the name because of the sexual abused they endured and the mysterious death of a student.

In 2005, the officials of the town of Goshen bulldozed the Haight Mansion citing it had structural damage. Except for the New State historical marker that was placed at the front gate, David Henry Haight's estate is only historical fact.

Haight-Browne Estate
1905 – 1921

Haight-Browne Estate
Goshen Public Library and Historical Society

After Mary Ellen Haight's death in 1895, the David H. Haight mansion was sold by the trustees who held the deed. The house, and 183 acres of property, was listed for sale on December 6, 1900, for $13,000. Maria and John McCullagh, and John's sister Miss Hamlin bought the property. They named the estate Low Wood Park. The property's name was recorded on the maps filed in the offices of Mr. Welsh and Mr. William Mayo.

John was a prominent New York City police chief whose reputation for law was well known. His expertise in law enforcement protocol was requested by many other police departments. On one occasion he traveled to Cuba and reorganized the police department of Havana, Cuba. In New York City he was superintendent of elections and was looking for a slower pace of life. He started a real estate business in New York and owned a private detective agency. He retired and moved to Goshen.

John owned several colts that he trained and drove on the Goshen historic track. His love of horses and competing in races was genuine.

One year after purchasing the property, John became sick and had a serious operation on his stomach. The day he returned home from the hospital, January 1, 1902, he died in his sleep. His wife Maria remained on the property for four more years. She could not maintain the estate and the property became shabby.

She sold the property in 1905 to Grant Hugh Browne, Vice-President of the United Lead Company, who named the estate Brownleigh Park. Haight was retained in the name of the property to be known as the Haight-Browne estate.

Browne was ambitious like David H. Haight and proceeded to bring the house and property back to its original condition and beyond. The restoration of the house and property was on a grand scale.

His first project was to restore the mansion to its previous style and grace. The mansion was enlarged and restored starting in 1905 and finished in 1920. He hired the best men of the building trades to restore the main building and to incorporate two outer buildings to the original. The quality of work of the tradesmen was precise and the additions were not discernible from the original building.

Reconstruction of the landscaping continued throughout the property. Many trees and shrubs were planted, making it an area to behold once again. The feeling of peace was felt throughout the property. Numerous bridle paths were added around the perimeter of the property and along East Division Road, known as Craigville Road today. Hillside grottos were added along the paths as a place for meditation. The public was invited to enjoy the paths and grottoes.

A new main gate was built to access the property at the corner of East Division Road and Main Street. The gates were massive. Its design was semicircular with four pillars two pillars were eighteen feet tall. Two ornamental iron gates, with rounded tops, were taller than the eighteen-foot pillars. They were fitted with two bronze plaques displaying a "B" for Browne. The gates are still there.

The farmland in the back of the house had not been maintained over the years and had fallen into deplorable condition. The wetlands reclaimed the fields making it waterlogged. Grant was a visionary and installed the first of its kind drainage system on a large area of land. Many residents watched the activity wondering if Grant would be successful. Dozens of men labored for the summer months installing drainage tiles underground to drain the land. The hours of work restored the area to its original condition of lush green lawns and farmland.

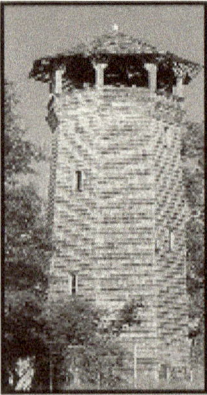

To have a constant water supply for the farm, a tall, large stout wood water tower with a cedar shake roof, was built on a knoll overlooking the land. It housed a large water reservoir. In later years when the water tower was no longer used, chimes were installed at the top of the tower that could be heard throughout the town of Goshen. It was named the Chime Tower.

New buildings were added to accommodate the lifestyle of Grant. A large two-story shingled structure was built in 1910 that was used as an equestrian show ring. He built a large barn to store his

Brownleigh Park Arena
Goshen Public Library and Historical Society

personal carriages and sulky carts. Next to the carriage house, a 120-foot stable was constructed to house his ponies that raced at the historic Goshen track. The loft of the stable stored hay, and a portion was finished with living quarters to accommodate the barn staff. Grant's most significant building was the Brownleigh park arena. It was an immense building with an indoor one-quarter mile track for horse racing.

He was a boxing enthusiast and regularly traveled to New York City to watch professional boxing matches. His love of boxing inspired him to turn the center of Brownleigh park arena into a boxing venue. The arena was the first of its kind in the area.

In 1913, just before World War I, Grant brought world class boxing matches to the arena. The matches would resemble those held at Madison Square Garden in New York City. He scheduled world class boxers bringing national attention and large crowds to Goshen. The arena was used for boxing matches but also to train boxers such as the top ranked Fred Fulton. In 1917 Les Darcy, "immortal of the ring," attracted the largest crowds to the arena. He was a young Australian who had won the 1908 world middleweight championship.

For eight years, Grant's boxing venues attracted many investors. He was pursued by Arcanum Attractions, a Hollywood movie company. In April 1921, he signed a ten-year contract. Arcanum Attractions would be producing movies replicating matches that had been fought at the arena. Goshen residents were saying that Hollywood had come to the East. The enthusiasm of the Hollywood East was short lived.

When World War I ended in 1919, the soldiers returning home caused an influx of civilians to the labor force. Unemployment, low wages, and a drop in agricultural prices caused a downturn in the stock market. The great depression started in 1920-1921; it resulted in the stock market dropping 45%. Many investors lost their fortunes that caused them to declare bankruptcy including Grant. In 1921 he declared bankruptcy and lost the estate to a group of New York City attorneys. He owned the property for a short 16 years.

In 1919 Grant Hugh Browne was charged with defrauding the

government by the U.S. circuit court of appeals in Cincinnati, Ohio. Grants illegal dealings with Germany resulted in a two-year sentence in federal prison at Leavenworth Kansas.

For two years, 1922 to 1923, the estate became an Army rehabilitation center for wounded soldiers returning from the war. In 1924, Henry Horkheimer purchased the property at a foreclosure sale. Four months later, Horkheimer sold the property to James Furey, a partner in a New York City attorney's group.

St. John Bosco's Salesian Fathers bought the property in May 1925 to be used as a seminary and youth summer camp. They paid $61,000.

Salesian School
HAIGHT PARK
1925 – 1985

1931 Salesian School
Goshen Public Library and Historical Society

After Grant Hugh Browne declared bankruptsy on Brownleigh park, the property went into foreclosure in 1922. The property languished on the market for three years until 1925 when St. John Bosco, Salesian Fathers, bought 52 acres for $61,000 dollars. The Roman Catholic order, dedicated to helping poor and abandoned children, opened a resident school for disadvantaged boys.

The Goshen location on the Haight estate, with its park-like landscaping, spascious lawns, athletic field and two ponds, would be a refreshing atmosphere for the boys attending the the school. "These beautiful surroundings (far from the noise and bustle of modern cities, in an environment of peace, tranquility and natural attraction) together with the Salesian Educative System of St. John Bosco, form a fine combination and offer an opportunity for boys to develop a solid religious and intellectual character."[1]

The Salesian fathers used the David Henry Haight mansion for the administrative offices, rectory, and dining hall. There was a small building to the left of the property that The Daughters of the Devin Zeal nuns used as their residence. The building was the caretakers cottage that David Henry Haight built on the property.

In 1931 Reverend Dominick Bottistello, the Father Director, supervised the construction of a new school, a three story brick building. The school was known as St. Michael's Institute, Salesian Junior Seminary, located at 334 East Main Street in Goshen. It was a large impressive building that housed the dormitory, classrooms, chapel, study hall, and gymnasium. During the school year, 40 students attended. A summer youth camp was held in the summer months with approximately 100 campers in attendance.

It was an afternoon in November 1939, 2:20 p.m. when William Kropp, a fireman living across the street at 359 Main street, heard a car horn blaring nonstop. He looked out his window to see flames shooting from the roof of the stables at St. Michaels school. He hailed a ride from a passinsg motorist to Main Street and Scotchtown Road to pull the fire alarm box. It took him a few minutes to return to the property to see the building was fully engulfed in flames.

The Dikeman Hose Company and the Cataract Engine and Hose Company responded to the fire alarm. Due to a misunderstanding, they went to the mansion where the administrative offices were located, laid a hose to the door, only to discover that the fire was down the hill at the two story 120 square foot stable. They went down the hill, laying two hoses from the stable pond to use on the fire. The pond was muddy and two firemen had to shovel the mud away from the intake screen on the hoses. After two hours of pumping, the pond was dry. The two hoses were ineffective and once the building

[1] Independent Republican, Thursday, February 15, 1951, page 9

collapsed, their mission was to contain the fire to the immediate area. The firemen were on the scene for three and one-half hours.

Farm hands, bystanders and firemen evacuated the stable and the only item that was lost was hay on the second floor. Six ponies, two horses, 100 chickens, and ducks were rescued from the first floor and 200 crates of onions from the second floor.

The probable cause of the fire were stumps burning nearby and it was thought the wind carried embers to the stable roof and ignited it. Father Bottistello thought it might have been a short in the electrical wire that ran between the stable and the arena building. The firemen packed up their hoses and gear and were preparing to leave around 4:00 p.m. When the firetrucks tried to back up the hill from the pond, the ground was saturated from the water and the firetrucks were stuck in the mud. The firemen tried to push the firetruck out of the mud but it would not budge. Mayor Walter G. Brown and Commissioner Joseph S. Coates, brought a village truck to tow the fire truck from the mud. It was successful, and the firetrucks were soon on Main Street.

The hay from the stable loft was still smoldering so Father Bottistello assigned one of the schools Brothers to check on the fire ravaged stable every 30 minutes. On one of the Brothers trips he discovered that the 200 hundred square foot wood shingled arena building was on fire. The second fire alarm was turned in at 10:15 p.m. The building was a total loss. Both buildings were underinsured and would be torn down.

St. Michaels, Salesian Junior Seminary School, presented itself in the town as an outstanding, wholesome religious experience for under-priviled boys. The school ran a summer camp every year and in 1964, 120 campers attended. There were all kinds of athletic activities, a pond to catch bullfrogs, swimming, and ponies and horses to ride. But for some, camp was a stressful time, especially for the younger boys. Paul Ramos was one of the campers that hated being there.

A tragedy happened at the school that would always be questioned and would designate the school as being haunted. August 9, 1964, 9-year-old Paul Ramos from New York City, died after falling 36 feet from a three story roof balcony. The case has never been solved although the tragedy has been investigated many times throughout the years.

The dormitories were on three floors supervised by a camp counselor. The younger boys were assigned to the third floor. They were constantly bullied by the older boys and the counselors ignored their behavior. A husky 14-year-old boy was relentless in harassing Paul. He would rummage through Pauls clothing chest and take what he wanted. On one occasion, the older boy took a silver buckle from Pauls clothing chest and kept it. The bully would tease and taunt Paul for his enjoyment never returning his belongings. In addition to being bullied, the campers had to contend with the Brother who was a pedophile. All the campers knew about him and felt uneasy in his presence, especially when they attended the Saturday night movies that he supervised. The boys motto: never be alone with him.

Thirty years later, two grown men, who were students at the school, came forward to talk about the sexual abuse they endured from two priests, Rev. George Puello and Rev. Richard Matikonas. The two priests would approach the boys in their dormatory beds at night and perform sexual acts on them against their will.

The third floor dormitory had an unsecured door that lead to the roof. The roof area was safe with a four to five foot parapet. The boys would go out there for fresh air and play their imaginary games. Paul wanted to be a pilot and pretended he was flying.

On the morning of August 9, 1964, the body of Paul Ramos, wearing pajamas and barefoot, was found on the pavement below. He fell 36 feet from the roof and died of a cracked skull. The Village of Goshen police were called to investigate the tragedy.

The police documented the area where Paul fell. Their first question, "Why was his body so far from the building?" If he jumped or fell from the roof his body would have been closer to the building. The investigation continued on the roof balcony. They searched for physical evidence such as skuff marks or other items but found nothing. Measurements were taken and confirmed that the parapet around the roof was four to five feet high in some places. The height of the wall ruled out that Paul jumped. They also ruled out suicide, sleeping walking, or that Paul was on the wall, lost his balance and fell. Was he thrown off the wall? The time of his death came into question. The local coroner noted that it was between 6 a.m. or 7 a.m. A forensic pathologist stated it was more likely around midnight.

The police started taking statements but their investigation was hampered by uncooperative employees, campers and counselors who left immediately without being questioned and others who refused to be questioned. Office records were missing or incomplete. They did find a report of his father telling the Brothers that a 14-year-old boy picked on his son and took his silver buckle. The buckle was not among Paul's belongings but mysteriously appeared on Paul's bed the day after he died. The police wanted to talk with the older camper. His name was never revealed; he left the school and was never found.

The schools enrollment declined and the facility closed in the fall of 1985. It continued to operate as a youth center until 1991 when the youth center closed.

The mansion on the property was not secured for 20 years and became a target for vandals. The house was demolished in 2008 after one side of the house collapsed. Saint Michaels School was torn down in the summer of 2022. A graveyard grotto and an alter built into the landscape are all that remain of the Salesian school.

Flicker, July 2, 2008

The Salesian property was put up for sale in 1991. It had amassed 1.7 million in back taxes. Orange County purchased the property at a tax forclosure sale. They had a vision to develop the property but that never materalized. The new Goshen Public Library and Historical Society was built on five acres of the property. Residents can enjoy the many walking paths throughout the park.

Numerous visitors and students have stated that they have experienced paranormal activity in the school building and grounds. Below are some of their accounts.

An adult took his friend to vist the school to reminisce about his days at summer camp. Standing by the side of the building the air was suddenly cold, when they witnessed smoke like figures jumping off the roof and landing near the basement door. They will never return.

A teenager, who was trespassing, described what he felt. It's a fucked up creepy place with a strong amount of negative energy.

Campers and several others saw an image of Paul Ramos on two occasions. Their dormatory was on the third floor near the door to the balcony. The door was always locked but on cold dark nights the door would suddenly open. The third floor was a spooky place.

Wanting to document the Salesian school and grounds, a photographer, at 8 a.m. on a Sunday morning, set up his tripod and began taking pictures. He was at the pond when all of a sudden he felt the presence of someone. He turned around and no one was there. Later he found out that he was by the old crypt where others had felt negative energy.

Another person described his encounter. This place is super creepy. I saw shadows moving across the lawn after dark, and heard whispers that gave me a skeevy feeling.

Across the street from the school, a family with two children, experienced haunting images. The children became disturbed at night after seeing a man dressed in black, dancing on the wall. They also saw a yellow blob.

On a sunny afternoon, before the school was demolished, I walked down the pavement to see the building up close. The tall building was intimidating with weeds, sapling trees and vines growing everywhere making it look sinister. The missing glass on the windows looked like infinite black holes. I stood there for a few minutes and felt the negative energy. The building was indeed haunted.

Case Cemetery
1760 – 1872

A SIGNIFICANT PIECE OF GOSHEN'S HISTORY

For over two hundred and fifty years the headstones with their epitaphs stood as guardians to protect and identify their contents below. The Case Cemetery, obscured from the public's view by dense overgrowth, and dead trees, was located twenty feet from a busy road, Sarah Wells Trail, Goshen, New York. I drove by this spot every day missing the old historical cemetery with its headstones standing as sentries waiting to be discovered.

One summer afternoon, I was waiting for traffic to pass to exit the driveway of Old Field Farm. Directly across from the driveway I questioned why a plot of land one hundred by two hundred feet was overgrown when the properties on either side had neatly mowed lawns. I had to investigate this odd phenomenon. I parked my car in the driveway and walked across the road.

Walking on the lawn of a neighbor, I went over to the area where the border of overgrowth started and stepped into the knee-high weeds. I was amazed at what I saw. It was an old cemetery long forgotten. The dates on the headstones were incredibly old, from the 1700 to the 1800 hundreds. A few stones were broken, others were sinking into the ground, but thirty-five stones were upright with readable names and dates.

It was in deplorable condition and on the verge of disappearing forever. It needed restoration immediately. I discussed my findings with a friend who previously did research on the Case Cemetery. She had submitted documentation to the town of Goshen board on

January 11, 2010, asking them to provide maintenance for the property. Ten years later, nothing was done.

The property was originally known as Elizabeth Hill and today it is Casetown. This plot of land was set off by the will of Daniel Case dated September 3, 1760, probated May 10, 1761. The deed of Eneas Case to James Carpenter is in the Orange County Clerk's office in Goshen.

Curious about such an old cemetery, I did research on the Case family name. During the French and Indian war of 1756, Goshen was the headquarters where soldiers assembled and resupplied before heading out into the territory. In January 1757, Colonel Benjamin Tusten, Captain Daniel Case and Captain J. Bull donated funds to build block houses #1 and #2 on the western frontier. A headstone for Captain Daniel Case who died in 1793, is in this cemetery. This is a historical cemetery with great significance of our forefathers.

Pioneer families built their homesteads in the same general area as a means of defense and survival. Three of the original Case properties are nearby and belong to private citizens.

I contacted the Goshen Historical Society looking for information about the names on the headstones. They gave me a list of thirty-five names, with dates, of those buried there. One stone was a testimony of filial affection to Abijah Wells.

To the memory of Abijah Wells – who died
February 1, 1821, A.D. aged 68 years.
(Gravity, Simplicity, a disinterested benevolence,
distinguishing characteristics.)
[His wife was Phebe Coleman. Epitaph omitted]
(Yet he trusted not in these for acceptance with God
– but only in the righteousness and merits the Lord
Jesus Christ.)
Reader "There is none other name under heaven
given among men whereby we must be saved."
(Acts. 4-12)

Abijah Wells Testimony of Filial Affection
Photo: Sandra Rothenberger

The names and dates of those buried in the Case Cemetery.
Daniel Case d. 1793, his wife Julia d. February 8, 1872, age 84 years 8 months 19 days

Daughter Sarah E. d. May 17, 1812, in the second year of her life

Son Wilmot d. May 11, 1823, age 12 years

Daughter Juliette d. August 26, 1824, in the first year of her life

Son David d. November 2, 1830, in his 76th year of his life

Son Virgil B. d. January 23, 1832, age 23 years 10 months

Son Jesse d. April 6, 1845, age 31 years

Daughter Phebe C. (Case) d. November 27, 1855, age 36 years

    Phebe was the wife of John N. Budd

Son Daniel Case d. May 1, 1857, age 77

David Case (son of Daniel Case) d. November 2, 1830, his wife Mary (Mary Wells) d. June 29, 1830, in the 81st year of her life

Son David Case Jr. d. March 11, 1816, age 36 years

Julianer his wife d. June 2, 1851, 68 years 3 months 6 days

Son Birdseye d. December 21, 1862, aged 77 years 4 months 21 days

Catherine his wife d. April 9, 1848, aged 61 years

Sarah Case, (daughter of Samuel) d. May 17, 1795, 66th year

Zacheus Case (son of Daniel D. 1716) d. January 9, 1822, aged 81 years 1 month 24 days

Son John d. January 24, 1826, aged 41 years 24 days

Daughter Hannah d. September 12, 1823, aged 37 years 7 months

George T. Case and his wife Elizabeth

Son Albert H. d. September 21, 1855, 1 month

Walter Anderson d. June 26, 1859, age 53 years 3 days, his wife was Frances

Son John B. d. July 21, 1851, aged 5 years

William B. and his wife Catherine B. McCoy

Son Andrew J. d. January 5, 1851, age 4 months

Daughter Catherine J. d. June 25, 1851, aged 1 year 2 months

Alexander McVey, his wife Martha d. May 1, 1838, aged 33 years, 3 months and 5 days

Alexander and Amelia McVey

Son George Horton, d. April 4, 1843, 2 years 8 months and 10 days

Ireal L. and his wife Louisa Slaight

Daughter d. January 7, 1842, aged 2 years, 9 months, and 10 days

Olive (Belknap) d. September 19, 1839, in the 42nd year of her life

Olive was the wife of Nathan H. Corwin

Elizabeth Belnap d. October 4, 1865, aged 66 years 10 days

Noah Carpenter d. March 1, 1847, aged 70 years

Wm. H. Gowers d. September 30, 1852, aged 28 years 10 months

Jane Gowers d. June 9, 1860, aged 38 years

Son James B. d. June 27, 1846, aged 15 years 3 months 14 days

Son James H. d. February 16, 1851, aged 4 months

Son William H. Jr. d. October 28, 1855, aged 3 years 9 months

John and his wife Ann Romain

41

The oldest headstones on the left side are the Case family burials
Photo: Sandra Rothenberger

Right side of the cemetery of other family burials
Photo: Sandra Rothenberger

I adopted the project to save this French and Indian War cemetery before it disappeared. At the next town of Goshen board meeting, I asked Supervisor Doug Bloomfield if he had any history about the Case Cemetery. His response was "no." I asked if the town would restore the cemetery and would he authorize the maintenance department to clean up the property. He said it was not the town's responsibility; the upkeep was the descendants' problem. "Who owns the cemetery?" No answer.

Searching the government's website Image Mate, it listed the cemetery as abandoned. Next town board meeting I asked who was responsible for an abandoned cemetery; the board shrugged their shoulders. Bloomfield reminded me that he would not authorize the town maintenance crew to do any work on the Case Cemetery. His definitive answer about restoration of the cemetery: "the towns money is for the residents." Afterwards, I felt those souls in that cemetery were the first "residents" of Goshen.

A week later I received a letter from Bloomfield, and he made it clear that we would not get one penny or any help from the town for the upkeep of the property. He suggested that we get the Boy Scouts to clean up the cemetery as a badge project.

Was Bloomfield wrong about the town's responsibility of upkeep for this cemetery? I attended the next board meeting to discuss law 97-54 with the board. When I made my presentation, the board was unaware of the law. They looked it up and read it to the audience. The four board members agreed that the law covered maintenance. Then Bloomfield said the law was to protect cemeteries, with a buffer, from encroachment by developers. He adjourned the meeting without further comment from any of us.

I sent four "Letters to the Editor" of local newspapers and there were two other feature articles published. I wanted the residents of Goshen to know that the town board would not appropriate any money to the restoration of a historical cemetery.

Times Hearld-Record, Residents call on Goshen to care for historic cemetery, Daniel Axelrod, June 22, 2020.
Goshen Independent, Abandoned Case Cemetery, Sandra Rothenberger, June 24, 2020.

Times Herald Record, Goshen lax in preserving historic ceme-tery, Sandra Rothenberger, June 25, 2020.

The Chronicle, Restoration of the Case Cemetery, Sandra Rothenberger, September 28, 2020.

Goshen Independent, Restoration of the Case Cemetery, Sandra Rothenberger, September 28, 2020.

After my disappointment with the town board, I contacted Village Historian Edward P. Connor to enlist his help. I asked Ed how we could get help from the town. His response was disappointing. We would get zero help and funds from the town as he and many others had appealed to the town for help before. There are 23 cemeteries in Goshen. Five are public. That leaves 18 historical cemeteries in desperate need of restoration. I only wanted to restore one.

One afternoon I saw the Village Historian, Edward P. Connor, working in the cemetery. He brought his push lawnmower and was cutting down the weeds. I stopped to give him moral support. We talked about cemeteries and his information about headstones was amazing.

The headstones were of several types:

- Slate 1650-1900. A metamorphosis of shale that was the earliest stone used extensively in American gravestones. This material was durable.

- Sandstone 1650-1890. Also called brownstone, is compressed sand that is not durable and deteriorates quickly.

- Marble 1780-1930. Also called limestone, is compressed shells. It was the material most desired in old cemeteries because of its pure white color and satin finish.

- Granite 1860-current day. Igneous rock is the strongest and most durable stone that exists today. The weather does not affect the stone or the engravings.

Gravestones always faced towards the road. Old cemeteries had a headstone and a small stone at the foot called footstones, indicating the top and bottom of the grave. Some children did not receive a headstone but only a large rock to mark their graves. Some received no stone, and these were the sunken areas in the ground. Headstones can be cleaned, but it is an expensive time-consuming process. There are procedures to upright the stones that have fallen or are severely leaning. The headstones are heavy, and it takes a strong person to upright them. Ed propped up the few sections of broken wood fence across the front of the cemetery and gave it a coat of white paint.

Clean up
Photo: Sandra Rothenberger

Debra Corr of Old Field Farm was annoyed that Bloomfield would not spend any time or money on this project. Her concern, as well as mine, was this historical cemetery would disappear. She scheduled a major cleanup of the fallen tree limbs and piles of rubbish. This was done at her own expense. Using her Skid Steer, a tractor and wagon, one of her farm hands, a Goshen trustee Kenneth Newbold and myself, we removed load after load of debris. We uncovered more stones and unmarked graves. One small headstone was imbedded in a tree trunk.

We surveyed the two large trees that were planted near each other and over the years had almost grown together. One was leaning precariously over the headstones. If it fell, the headstones would be crushed, and nothing would be left but rubble. The next violent thunderstorm could be the one we all dreaded. Debra contacted an arborist to give us a quote to remove the tree. It was $1,200 and not an expense we should be paying out of our pockets. We were hoping for a good Samaritan.

A local newspaper, *The Chronicle*, contacted me and wanted to do a feature article about our efforts to save the cemetery. Ed Connor and I were interviewed. An article was published in *The Chronicle*, Pick up a rake, a shovel or a check book, Geri Corey, June 26-July 2, 2020. There were numerous comments from the public.

The newspaper articles drew the attention of the Industrial Development Agency (IDA), and they contacted Debra Corr. They wanted her to apply for a Project Expenditure from the Orange County Funding Corporation and if approved for a grant, we would receive $1,200 for the removal of the old tree. I put together a six-page application and submitted it to the IDA board. It was the middle of July when we received news that we would be getting the funds. This was our good Samaritan.

In September 2020, John W. Younie, an arborist, of Arbor Valley Tree, Inc., set a date to remove the tree. Several neighbors were there to watch. It would be interesting how a one-hundred-foot old tree would be removed without any damage to the headstones.

Arbor Valley Tree, Inc.
Photo: Sandra Rothenberger

The large bucket truck slowly backed into the cemetery and lowered the outriggers for stability. An inspection of the safety equipment was done before being used. The sound of the chainsaw pierced the silence, indicating the project had started.

John Younie started at the lowest limb of the tree. He would secure a branch with ropes, cut it with the chainsaw and lower it to the ground. When the bucket truck was fully extended at the top of the tree, he turned off the chainsaw. He attached several thick ropes to the large tree trunk, verified procedures with his man on the ground and lowered the ropes. Several minutes passed before the first chainsaw cut. Then the chainsaw stopped. Younie looked over the large tree trunk, coordinated with his man on the ground, and again surveyed where the tree trunk would fall. The chainsaw started, his helper pulled the ropes tight, and the top of the tree fell. It hit the ground with a thud and never touched a headstone. We all cheered and took many pictures.

The view of the cemetery was amazing. Now that the cemetery was visible from Sarah Wells Trail, there were many comments. "We never knew a cemetery was there."

Covid 19 took over our lives in October 2020 and all work on the cemetery stopped. It saddens me that the town of Goshen does not want to preserve its history.

Dutchess Quarry Caves
1974 NATIONAL REGISTER OF HISTORIC PLACES

In 1963 the New York State Archaeology Society discovered Ice Age caves on the northwest face of Mount Lookout, a 580-foot mountain located at Route 17A and Quarry Road in Goshen, New York. Two years later in 1965, Archaeologists George Walters, Bill Ehlers and Bill Vernooy searched the caves to find fossils. They found 5 fluted points used for hunting, Paleo-Indian hearths with bits of charcoal, fire-cracked rocks, caribou bones, and lumps of red ocher, a mineral used as a pigment. There were 30 artifacts found. The New York State Museum in Albany dated the bones using a radiocarbon process to be 13,800 years old.

In the last Ice Age, 11,500 years ago, the Paleo-Indians arrived in North America. They were the first inhabitants of America. Giant ice sheets opened in Alaska and Alberta, Canada, making it possible for Ice Age inhabitants to migrate from Asia and Siberia. A land bridge called Beringia was used to cross the Bering straits from Siberia to Alaska.

Fluted points

They wore warm animal hides and brought their tools with them to hunt large animals from Mount Lookout. Their tools for hunting were distinctive fluted points made of stone, ivory, or bone. The fluted points made it possible to date their arrival on the East Coast. Goshen is home to the oldest Paleo-Indian site east of the Mississippi.

The Paleo Indians lived in small nomadic groups in an area where there was sufficient food to feed their families. From the top of Mount Lookout, they had a view of the submerged cedar swamp where abundant game roamed. They hunted mastodon, caribou, and giant beaver, killing them with their fluted points, secured to a spear. The game would be taken to one of eight caves where it would be prepared to eat.

The submerged cedar swamp where the Paleo Indians hunted would become the Black Dirt region in Goshen. Millennium ago, the swamp was fertile sapric soil from an ancient glacial lake bottom. The land was transformed from a swamp to a marsh by decades of flooding from the Wallkill River. The "Drowned Lands of the Wallkill" was converted into fertile black soil in the 1880's by Polish and Volga Germans. They constructed drainage culverts that formed the Cheechunk Canal and made it possible to farm the rich soil of the land.

Orange County has owned Mount Lookout land since the 1830's. In 1937, John Arborio, the owner of Dutchess Quarry and Supply Company, Pleasant Valley, New York, leased 49.6 acres of land on Quarry Road in Goshen to mine dolomite (stone). After 30 years, and the discovery of Dutchess Quarry Caves on Mount Lookout in 1960, the company wanted to purchase the land instead of leasing. They submitted their proposal to Orange County but were denied. It was a concern to the County that additional blasting would degrade the integrity of the caves.

In 1982 Orange County leased an additional 55 acres of land to Dutchess Quarry and Supply Company for a total of 104.6 acres. For eighty years Dutchess Quarry and Supply operated its mining operation with little oversight from Orange County or the Town of Goshen. As a result, significant destruction occurred to Mount Lookout historical caves on the southwest side.

March 23, 2013, Peckham Materials Corporation leased the quarry. Peckham removed the stone from the mine for eight years before Tilcon leased the land in 2021.

Tilcon offers crushed stone, sand, gravel, hot mix asphalt and ready-mix concrete. Their operation has been a nightmare for those who live in the area. There is a development of expensive houses on Quarry Road and constant blasting has destroyed the integrity of the houses. The blasting noise is deafening not only to humans but their pets. The crushing of the stone creates a gritty, thick gray cloud that travels for some distance. Nothing is spared from the dust, it coats the houses, lawns, cars, fields, and roads and finds its way into the houses. When they are making asphalt for paving the roads, the hot tar smell makes people sick. At the end of Quarry Road is the Valley View Nursing Home and Hearthstone senior apartments. These seniors are already compromised, and the air quality is harmful. Neighbors have complained about this to the County and the town. They say they cannot do anything.

Tilcon has tried to alleviate the gray dust problem by spraying water on the stone crusher and on the road. Their efforts are minimal only by clearing the dust cloud around the quarry and creating gray slush on the road. Tilcon blasting and extracting the stone has created a 300-foot deep mine next to Mount Lookout. The caves on the southwest side of the mountain have been destroyed by Tilcon.

Tilcon Quarry 300-foot-deep mining site

In 1970, Orange County established a 2-acre buffer on the northwest side of the caves. The site was listed on the National Register of Historic Places in 1974, requiring a buffer of 13.2 acres. Another easement of 20 acres was added in 2016 creating a buffer of 34.6 acres.

Tilcon offered $500,000 to Orange County to purchase additional land around the mine. County officials were receptive to the offer but would create a 100-foot buffer around the 17 acres they owned to preserve the caves. Leadership was lacking with the County and the town of Goshen; the sale expired. Three years later in 2020, the County lawmakers voted 14-7 to solicit bids for the property. County Officials revised the offer with a reduction in land to 31 acres and an increase in the price to $1.3 million.

Several historical associations took action to spread the word about the importance of these caves. Mike Edelman, Orange Environment, held a news conference to discuss how to protect the Dutchess Quarry Caves. The group included Chief Vincent Mann of the Turtle Clan of the Ramapough-Lenape tribe of Native Americans. These caves are sacred grounds to them having been an early encampment of Native Americans. The group was advocating in developing a master plan.

Payment to the Town of Goshen for the leased land is based on the amount of stone that was mined. Over the years, income has dropped significantly. Legislature Chairman Steve Brescia was in favor of selling saying the taxpayers would benefit from the $1.3 million dollars versus the lease payments. Legislator Jeffery Berkman wants the sale to go forward which would hold Tilcon responsible for reclamation of the area if they vacated the property. John McCarey, Director, Orange County Real Property was quoted as saying in The Epoch Times, "I think we'd better off to get rid of it from a county point of view."

Liability for the property of the caves is the responsibility of Orange County. It is of great concern if someone falls off a cliff into a retention pool and drowns. Substantial fencing has been discussed. If Tilcon vacates the leased property, the 300-foot-deep mine will need a pump running constantly to drain the ground water. If the dolomite mine is filled with water, engineers say there is a possibility the water would weaken the limestone caves, and a disastrous collapse of Mount Lookout could occur.

The Dutchess Quarry Caves are documented as extremely important in the society of archaeologists, anthropologists, historians, and many residents of the town. Goshen is the location of the first inhabitants on the east coast in America. Mount Lookout Caves should be preserved forever but there is a possibility they may be destroyed.

Goshen prides itself on having a historical town, but when it comes to taking action to preserve history, the town is silent. They form committees that take no action. The caves were discovered in 1965. The town should have stopped all mining of Mount Lookout that year instead of leasing more land. They let it be mined to the present day, and now they have the problems of a 300-foot hole.

Mount Lookout Caves are important to everyone in the United States. This is the location of the first inhabitants of America.

Orange County not to renew Dutchess Quarry mining permit
"County Executive Steven Neuhaus said he is pulling the plug on the operations when the current contract expires."
https://midhudsonnews.com, 9/10/2024

Haunted Farmhouse

HARRIMAN DRIVE, GOSHEN, NEW YORK

Kafziel/Gallery, Wikimedia Commons

The decaying ghostly white farmhouse with red shutters, stood there extruding evil. It was the location where a serial killer, for five hours, tortured two women to death. The house was located on a dead-end tractor path hidden from view by years of overgrowth. The farmhouse, with a frontage of 300 feet and a swamp on one side of the house, was located on Harriman Drive, Goshen, New York.

When I moved to Goshen, my family warned me not to drive down Harriman Drive to look at the farmhouse saying it was not safe.

There were rumors of motorcycle gangs gathering at the dead-end road to party, and others engaged in nefarious activities in the crumbling farmhouse. I did not heed their warning, and one day drove down Harriman Drive to look at the farmhouse. My senses were on alert; my heart was beating fast but I continued my journey.

The road was full of potholes with deep ditches and wetlands on both sides. Not a road I should be driving down in a Honda Accord. I drove slowly and in a few minutes I stopped in front of the farmhouse. Chills ran down my spine and the house had an aura that was frightening. I briefly viewed the house and property, turned around and I left the ghastly farmhouse behind.

When talking with friends about my adventure of driving to the farmhouse they said there was another house at the dead end of the road. Curiosity was my invitation to go back.

It was a sunny summer day when I turned from the main road onto Harriman Drive. I closed my windows, locked my doors, and put on the AC. The road past the farmhouse had more potholes. To avoid getting a flat tire, I drove in the potholes slowly. The overgrowth was encroaching onto the road, and it was remarkably close to my car. It was like driving in a tunnel. Soon I could see a clearing at the end of the road. I came to the dead end and stopped. To my right was a small two-story farmhouse with the windows boarded up and a padlock on the front door. There was a rusty van parked on the side of the house. Trash was strewn all over the front yard. Enough evidence for me to believe that people had been back there recently.

Yikes, what have I gotten myself into. My head started to pound, and I began to sweat. I took a quick look around my car, made a fast 3-point turn and got out of there. I was frightened, not of the dead but of the living, and it was agony having to drive slowly. Once on the main road I told myself I would never go back.

Locals were telling stories that inside the house, voices of women saying "help me" could be heard and visions of tortured women appeared on the walls and floating through the air. The souls of Angelina Hopkins and Brenda L. Whiteside haunted the house because of their horrible deaths.

From various accounts and pictures, the inside of the house had rotten floorboards with holes to fall through, a half-collapsed staircase to the second floor, and parts of the ceiling had fallen to the floor to block the path. There were holes in the walls, all the windows were broken, graffiti was everywhere, and it was filled with trash and garbage. Not a safe place to be walking around.

Although Goshen would prefer not to be in the limelight, the story was talked about for many years in the town and the surrounding areas. But the haunting visions and voices did not chase everyone away. It beckoned to ghost hunters and paranormal groups who wanted to experience supernatural visions and sounds themselves.

In 2007, the first group came to investigate the "spooky house." Looking at the house they described it as creepy and going into the house they felt a presence of evil, pain and sadness.

They looked at the pictures they had taken and listened to the voice recorder. The pictures showed "orbs," and the tape had swishing sounds that sounded angry. They left.

The second group had little resolve. Before entering the house, they heard whispers coming from the swamp. They freaked out and left in a hurry. Nothing like whispers from a swamp to frighten you.

The third group that came were professionals compared to the other two groups. They came with digital cameras, video cameras and several flashlights. They explored every room on the first and second floors, always feeling a sinister presence. The wind was blowing through the broken windows making it bone chilling cold.

Two men volunteered to go down to the basement. A fully charged video camera would not work in the basement. They left feeling overwhelmed with the evil presence of the house.

The next day, the group viewed the photos and video on the digital camera. An apparition of a girl was on the wall, and listening to the recording, they had gotten what sounded like a girl saying, 'Help Me.' The group described the farmhouse as extremely haunted, and whatever is there, was not friendly or happy. The group never returned to the house again.

For 35 years the house sat empty and became more deteriorated and shabbier looking. Weeds overtook the property and the trees around the house had died and were in various stages of rotting. Shutters were falling off; the front door was stuck open hanging by one hinge. It would have been a great movie scene in a Steven King movie. It is likely that a few brave teenagers made it an adventure to visit the house. The rooms inside had been vandalized and defaced throughout the years.

The house sat on a tiny piece of land of 523 acres. In 2015 Legoland/Merlin Entertainments bought the property to construct an amusement park. Legoland learned that the deteriorating farmhouse on the property was the dumping ground of serial killer Nathaniel White and was haunted. Legoland representatives were spooked by the history of the house.

On July 15, 2015, in the middle of the night the farmhouse burnt down.

Inns of Goshen

Goshen is home to two 1700's historical inns. The 1747 Stagecoach Inn, and the 1790 Orange Inn. Each Inn has its own distinctive character, and the history of each is nothing like the other for the last 283 years.

ANTHONY DOBBINS STAGECOACH INN
1747

268 Main Street

The Inn was built in 1747 using timber from the surrounding land. Anthony Dobbins bought the three-acre property in 1791, to raise Merino and Saxony sheep. He observed many coaches cutting through his property to Albany Post Road. Being resourceful and seeing an opportunity to start a business, he opened his home as an inn, Dobbins Stagecoach Inn. The Inn was a successful business, and many coaches stopped for refreshments. Notable people as Governor

George Clinton ate there, and Justices from the courthouse took their dinner breaks at the Inn. By 1801 it was a thriving business; started by coaches cutting across his property.

Henry Astor of Long Island bought the famous English thoroughbred Messenger in 1793. Messenger would be available for stud services at different farms in New York. In 1801, Anthony Dobbins offered Messenger for stud service in his barn, and his son Abadallah was sired in 1823. The blood line of Abadallah sired Hambletonian who became the sire of all Standardbreds. Hambletonian's notoriety of sulky racing established the Goshen Historic Track as the "trotting horse mecca."

Anthony Dobbins died in 1818 and was buried in Slate Hill Cemetery. He left the Inn to his second wife Nancy Ann Board Dobbins. Nancy Ann bequeathed the property to her nephew John J. Heard in 1857. He lived at the Inn with his widowed mother since 1812. He enlarged the Inn by adding a wood addition to the brick structure. The edition of the October 26, 1830 paper had a for sale ad for Merino and Saxony Sheep. The sheep were from the original herd of Anthony Dobbins.

Nicholas Franchot bought the Inn as an investment in 1915 from Fanny and Eliza Heard. Fifteen years later Franchot sold the Inn to his daughter Janet and her first husband, William Hickok IV. The Inn was their private residence that they enlarged and restored. It is rumored that William Hickok IV was a direct descendant of the family line of James Butler "Wild Bill" Hickok.

Janet Hickok divorced and lived in the house until her death in 1965. Many townspeople knew her generosity; she donated to many causes. Janet Hickok's son from her first marriage, William Hickok V., and his wife Marjorie (Margo) Miller moved into the house in 1965 and used it as their residence.

Margo was a model in New York City and came to Goshen to attend a party at the Westinghouse Estate, owned by the Gabor sisters. She met her husband William at the party.

In 1985, after 20 years of residing in the Inn, Margo and William opened the Dobbins Stagecoach Inn as a Bed & Breakfast. William died in 1987; Margo continued to run the Inn. Margo was a perfect hostess and enjoyed telling the history of the Inn and show-ing her many antiques. Margo George Hickok passed away in 2011. Ownership of the Inn was passed to her children who listed the Inn for sale in 2014. The Inn had been in the Hickok family for 110 years.

In 2014 Faith Ferguson and her husband Ron Boire purchased the Inn. They restored the Inn to its original condition. Restoration was a two-year project. The Inn opened in 2016 offering Hudson Valley the finest guest rooms, restaurant, and intimate event venues.

It is a fact that old historical houses have friendly ghosts, and the Stagecoach Inn is no exception. Rocking chairs would move with no external force, the placement of furniture would be slightly altered, and occasionally there was a ghostly appearance or two. Ghosts are the charm of old houses.

ORANGE INN
1790

159 Main Street, Goshen

The Orange Inn is famous for its part in the Revolutionary War when the basement was used as a jail. The notorious Claudius Smith, a marauding loyalist, was terrorizing the countryside by robbing the rich and giving the stolen goods to the poor. After many months he was finally caught. He was held in the Inns basement prison. His punishment given by the courts for his crimes was death by hanging. He was hanged in the Presbyterian Church Park.

The Inn was a tavern with rooms to rent. Many dignitaries, actors, sports icons, and famous people visited the Inn's bar for refreshments. On harness racing day, patrons from the Goshen Historic Track overwhelmed the Inn. Goshen's Historic Track was established in 1838, and the town would be overflowing with people on race day. Pari-mutuel betting on the races drew people from around the county. The bar would be packed with men celebrating their wins or losses. The police were busy keeping the rowdy crowds in check; there would be arguing and drunk patrons in the bar.

John P. LaBurt, Jr., his wife Phyllis Aldecoa LaBurt, son John P. LaBurt III, and two daughters, Fern Farley and Mimi LaBurt, owned the Orange Inn since 1958. For twenty years they had overwhelming crowds at the Inn on race day. Attendance at the track decreased dramatically when the late Roland Harriman outlawed Pari-mutuel betting in 1978. The Harriman Family and the Orange County Driving Park Association held the stewardship of the track for 85 years. In 1979, responsibility for the track was transferred to Goshen Historic Track Inc.

When betting stopped at the track, the massive crowds of patrons at the Orange Inn dwindled. Fern Farley found it difficult to keep the Inn with business in decline. Upkeep of the Inn was nonexistent, and the building became shabby. They decided it was time to sell the Inn.

Luigi and Victor Kapiti from Pearl River, New Jersey, bought the Inn in August 2006 paying Mimi LaBurt $1.3 for the building at 159 Main Street. Kapiti promised that the run-down restaurant, bar, and studio apartments would be restored. He invested $700,000, changed the name to Limoncellos, and revised the menu to offer Northern Italian cuisine. Limoncellos would be an Italian family restaurant. The restaurant's fresh look and menu appealed to the people of Goshen and at times was totally booked.

In 2021 Luigi and Victor Kapiti announced they would be converting Limoncellos into a boutique hotel. Their idea would be to create a boutique hotel that they saw in Europe. It was a project that took two years to complete and was done during the 2-year COVID epidemic. The Inn was gutted from top to bottom that stripped away its history. The interior became a new white shiny look. Floors were added to accommodate the 31 luxury apartments. The exterior changed and today it looks like a new white modern building. The Orange Inn was gone after 232 years.

A building 232 years old has its share of paranormal activities. Diners would see visions of women floating in the air and on the walls in the dining room. The basement, under the bar, is a foreboding place to avoid. Its dark, and damp air gives those walking around a chill. Tunnels and cell sized rooms are reminiscent of the jail that was used in the Revolutionary War.

Steve Joy, the caretaker of the upstairs rooms, tells his story of ghosts. Joy lives in a room at the Inn. One evening there was a knock on his door; he opened it, and no one was there. This happened several times. Finally, he opened the door, said an expletive and "cut that out" and he never heard it again.

GOSHEN INN
1910, ORANGE COUNTY HUNT CLUB

40 Park Place

Building the Goshen Inn had been discussed for some time by the Directors of the Orange County Hunt Club. The intent was to build a clubhouse to resemble the houses in Melton, Mowbry, the fox hunting center of England. The architects of Walker & Gillette were retained. The pattern of the brickwork was unique in the early 20th century as it is today. To obtain the color and texture of the brick, it went through a process called overburnt. Exterior architectural details and interior appointments followed the same English Inn style.

The property selected was located at 40 Park Place. The front of the building would face the Presbyterian Church green; the back yard was at the fence of the Goshen Historic Track.

The first floor would have a large dining room, smoking, billiards, lounging and reception rooms. The two upper floors would have 18 suites. The lawn area at the back of the house, was designed to have an English garden and a swimming pool.

In 1912 under the leadership of Mrs. E. H. Harriman and the residents of Tuxedo and Arden, construction of the Goshen Inn started. The cost of the building would be $100,000. Mrs. Harriman donated $25,000 with Robert Goelet and F. Howard Ford each donating $10,000. The stockholders of the Orange County Hunt Club would pay the remainder.

The Goshen Inn was damaged by a fire on August 5, 1921. The Harriman Estate and the Goshen Inn Company authorized V. D. Wallace to sell the property appraised for $49,000. In 1941 Carl and Walter Neithold and partner Richard Love bought the building and restored it.

Chester LeBaron, an entrepreneur, owned many properties in Goshen and bought the Goshen Inn in 1982. LeBaron promised the Neitholds he would maintain the buildings historic character. He was unable to keep his promise.

The building was damaged by a lightning strike, water and winds from Superstorm Sandy and the rising costs of taxes and water bills forced LeBaron to seek a tenant. Previously, LeBaron had leased the building to Bucci's, Oliver's and Park Place who kept the building's English character in place. The elaborate brickwork and angled Elizabethan roofs remained unaltered.

Joseph Betro wanted to purchase the building, not be a tenant. His intent was to renovate the building and open his restaurant Delancy's. The standoff lasted for two years when skyrocketing maintenance forced LeBaron to sell to Betro in 2009.

The restaurant was renovated at a cost of $200,000. New windows and French doors were added, the restaurant area was stripped of its Elizabethan character, and a new roof destroyed the angled Elizabethan roofs.

Another historic inn was lost to modern renovations.

Interpines Sanitarium
1867 – 1959

255 Main Street, Goshen, NY

Samuel Marsh was the interim president of the Erie Railroad until Robert Berdell was appointed president for the term of 1864-1867. Berdell came from New York City to build his house in Goshen. He purchased the site of the 1774 house of General George D. Wickham.

Berdell built a large expensive, very ornate mid-Victorian-style house. It was completed in 1867. Berdells ownership of the house was a short nine years ending in 1876. He had an altercation with two brothers of the Murray family ending with one of the brothers shot and killed. Berdell put the house up for sale and left Goshen. The house remained vacant for eight years. A caretaker took care of the property.

In 1889 Dr. F. W. Seward, Sr. bought the building, added a wing to the house, and opened the Interpines Sanitarium. The public referred to the building as "Dr. Seward's Home for Invalids." Seward thought the mansion would be a general care home, but it soon became a hospital for people with Disorders of the Nervous System.

In 1925 Seward Sr. died and his son Frederick W. Seward Jr. assumed the responsibility of running the hospital. He added a second wing to the building in 1925 to accommodate female patients. The new wing made it possible to accommodate fifty-six patients. The Cory building, a two-story structure, was built separately from the main house to accommodate male patients. They could access the main building by a half underground corridor. The sanitarium became one of the largest businesses in Goshen. Many residents of Goshen were employed by the hospital.

The sanitarium was known for its personal care and many people came from New York City and Northern New Jersey. They were healing their nervous ailments through quiet surroundings, rest, and a slower pace of living. The Sanitarium had a stellar reputation.

America's Civil War Joan of Arc hero Anna Elizabeth Dickinson was committed to Danville State Hospital for the Insane, West Pittston, Pennsylvania in February 1891. Susan, Anna's sister, stated that Anna was suffering from paranoia. Anna insisted she was not paranoid and asked to be transferred to Interpines Sanitarium in Goshen. Six months later in August she was back to lecturing.

Over the years new buildings were added, and the landscaped grounds were a parklike setting. There were four buildings situated on 19 acres. The nurses had their own residence with a six-car garage and laundry. The utilities building supplied steam and hot water. There were five structures from the original estate landscaping. A greenhouse, an aviary, an octagonal pigeon house next to the garage and two summer pavilions. The extensive gravel paths guided patients around the lawns with ponds, and flower gardens. Water lilies grew in three of the ponds, and a rock garden had a stream running through it.

The first floor of the mansion, with the original architectural details, was used by the staff and patients. The two parlors were lit by chandeliers; one room had a grand piano. Other rooms were a library, a sunroom, and a dining room with a view of the rose garden. One room was used as an office by the two doctors and a bookkeeper. There was also a switchboard and a tiny pharmacy. The second and third floors were used by female patients. Patients with serious problems were in a locked ward on the third floor.

The front of the property was one block wide. The entrance to the property was as grand as the mansion. The entrance was a long semicircular driveway lined with stone planters that had lights. The building could also be accessed by the front walk from Main Street. The front lawn had many large mature trees and a tennis court.

The Sanitarium closed in 1959 due to changing times in treating mental illness. The mansion was in a state of deterioration.

The buildings were razed in 1964 and the site scraped clean. The Orange County Government Center and a jail would be built here.

Mystery at Viking Hill Farm
TRANQUILITY OF THE FARM

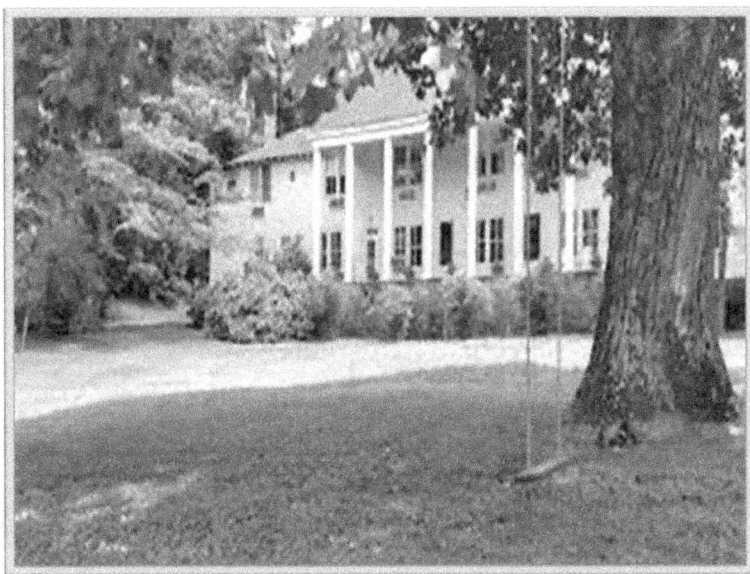

On the outskirts of the town of Goshen, New York, on Sarah Wells Trail, there is a beautiful equestrian facility known as Viking Hill Farm. Only the long winding driveway is visible from the road, old trees hide the estate.

Driving through the stone pillars, one will experience a calming effect that dissipates the hustle and bustle of life. Passing by a natural fed pond there may be egrets, ducks, or other wildlife. The driveway continues up a substantial hill, when an impressive 1834 restored farmhouse comes into view. Large columns surround the wraparound porch standing as guardians but also say welcome.

Proceeding along the drive, past three buildings, down the big hill, the equestrian center comes into view. There is an outdoor ring, an indoor ring and twenty-four stalls filled with show horses. To the riders, it is a home away from home with a tack/kitchen area, an office, trophy room and viewing room. The viewing room has two sofas, and a television. A row of chairs, across the front of the large windows, overlook the indoor arena to watch the riders put their horses through their paces.

Upon entering the barn, dogs, cats, people and sometimes a whinny from one of the horses greet you. There is a wonderful camaraderie among the boarders and riders, enhanced by the sweet smell of hay and horses.

A barn manager keeps the activity of riders at a smooth pace. Boarders come during the day to ride and exercise their horses. The young riders taking lessons try to keep their enthusiasm in check. The large outdoor arena is used in the summer, presenting a fluid motion of horse and rider. The owner, Leah Slate, keeps the activities of the barn humming along.

There is the usual flow of professionals coming to the barn such as farriers, veterinarians, and special trainers. Hay trucks, feed delivery trucks and horse trailers are a common sight. The area around the barn has twenty-four well-groomed paddocks, one for each horse to have its own grazing area.

During the day, resting in the shade by the house, Monarch butterflies and hummingbirds drink the nectar from the flowers. In the spring, the "peepers" (tiny frogs) emerge from the ponds to sing their song to attract a mate. Watching the sunsets and moon rising are pictures that can only be captured by the human eye. Once dark, the night animals emerge. The only disturbing sound is a large pack of coyotes howling at the back of the property by Purgatory Swamp.

It is inconceivable to think this relaxed way of life at this farm would become the scene of a disappearance, murder, or suicide of a person.

THE MYSTERY

This is the author's personal account of
The Mystery at Viking Hill Farm

Looking at a babbling brook one has a feeling of peacefulness. Looking at a swamp, your senses perceive a sinister and forbidden place. It is not the blue water of a stream you see but a stagnant pond of brown water with a quicksand bottom. It is a place to be avoided.

The Purgatory Swamp was at the back of the farm property. Everyone knew it was there, but no one gave it any thought. No one had any reason to go back there. This was the location where the mystery begins.

As the Slates had done before, they decided to take a long week-end vacation to a warm and sunny spot. The workers in the barn had their work schedule and the barn manager had a list of the things that needed to be taken care of. Leah asked me to stay at the house and take care of her four dogs. I had watched the house and dogs before.

The large old farmhouse reminded me of the one I had lived in when I was married. I would be comfortable with the squeaky floor-boards, things that rattled in the wind, and the steam heating system that banged and hissed when heating the old house. Old houses had their own personality and could be scary for a person who never lived in one.

Saturday, March 16th was the first night of my stay. The dogs had their routine of eating at 5:30 p.m., outside for a short walk, then back inside to sleep and snore in the living room. I also spent my evening in the living room watching a movie. Around 9:30 p.m. the dogs would nudge me to go outside before settling down for the night. The dogs were confined to the downstairs until their morning wakeup call at 5:30 a.m.

Sunday morning at 1:13 a.m. all the dogs started barking loudly. The deep bark of the Rottweiler resonated throughout the house jolting me awake. Thinking they heard night animals in the yard, I yelled at them to be quiet. They were quiet for 30 seconds before barking again. This time I went to the head of the stairs and yelled again for them to be quiet. There was a woof or two but eventually they settled down and I went back to bed. Little did I know they were trying to alert me to danger.

Leah came home on Tuesday and caught up on all the things that happened in the barn and house. When she asked about the dogs, I told her about them barking and waking me up early Sunday morning. She asked if I got up and looked out the windows to see what the dogs were barking at. I said no. Her reply, "Do not ever ignore their barking again; at least get up and look out the window." I would regret ignoring the dogs alert to look out the window.

Wednesday started just like every day. Everyone was busy doing their work and Leah was catching up on the activities of the barn for the last four days. The supervisor of the men that worked in the barn, had a wagon full of manure that needed dumping. He drove the tractor and wagon down the dirt road to the back of the property to dump the load. He had done this countless times.

Purgatory Swamp was within view of where he dumped the manure. He dumped the wagon and was looking around when he spotted a black SUV stuck in the mud up to the doors. It was hidden among the brush and trees. He stood there for a while waiting for someone to get out of the car or see them walking around. The only sound he heard was dead silence. With haste, he drove the tractor and wagon back to the barn.

He found Leah and excitedly told her of the black car stuck and hidden from view at the back of the property by the swamp. She was surprised that someone would drive their car to the end of the road and beyond until stuck. It had to be someone who did not know the property. Leah was concerned that someone was hurt and needed help.

She got her daughter and in a four-wheel drive vehicle drove down the dirt road to investigate. They stopped at the end of the road, within sight of the car and turned off the engine. They sat there for a minute looking for someone walking around. They called, "is anyone there" hoping to get a response. When no one responded they decided to approach the car with caution. Looking through the windshield they did not see anyone sitting in the front seat. They looked in the passenger window and saw papers scattered on the seat, children's clothing and a Victoria's Secret shopping bag. They thought maybe the car belonged to a woman with children. She looked in the back window, but it was too dark to see anything. Leah knew she should not touch the car but because of the children's clothing in the front seat she was concerned children could be on the floor. She opened the door and found the back seat empty.

With haste they returned to the barn to call the state police. Everyone was at the barn door waiting for their return. They were a captive audience listening carefully to hear the details. The car was stuck in the mud up to the frame by Purgatory Swamp, the items on the front seat, and no one around.

Then reality sets in with the riders. There were riding trails in that area that they all used.

They never had a sense of danger. They realized that a person walking out of the brush could have spooked the horses and the injuries they could have sustained. It would be a long time before the riders used those trails again.

In the evenings, some riders came to the barn to use the indoor ring that had bright lights. There were floodlights around the barn but beyond the circle of light it was pitch black. Riders were hesitant to come at night. Night check on the horses was done at 7 p.m. Those two people did their work in record time.

Leah rushed into the office where I was working. Quickly she told me of the events that happened by the swamp. Immediately she called the New York State Police. I was surprised that something like this could happen without anyone seeing something. There are many people around during the day that would question a car going down the dirt road. Then I remembered the Sunday morning the dogs were barking. They were trying to alert me that a car was in the driveway. Leah's words "at least get up and look out the windows" echoed in my head. If I had looked out the window I would have called the police, and this mystery would not have happened.

The police came to the office, and Leah explicitly told them that this incident was not to be in the papers. It would only bring people snooping around her property. I listened to her tell the police the story from the point where the farm worker discovered the car, the items in the car and that she had opened the back door.

The police asked to see the car. They drove down the dirt road and stopped at the edge of the muck. First, they searched the car and made an inventory of what was inside. They canvassed the area looking for clues. They were looking for clothing, someone who had fallen and was stuck in the mud, or footprints in the mud where they had walked away. They found nothing. Whoever was there just disappeared.

It was a big property with many buildings and the police wanted to search all of them. Searching in the barn first, the police looked in every stall, all the rooms and the loft. Then onto the pump house, the apartment, and the run-in sheds for the horses in each paddock. The house and two large buildings up the hill were not a place for someone to hide.

The police searched the property and found nothing. They suggested that the person could have walked across the fields and hid in the neighbor's barn. Leah called her neighbor, who was some distance across the field, gave her a summary of what had happened, and asked her to search her barns and outbuildings. She called back and said they found nothing.

Leah called her other neighbor who told her he was in Florida on vacation. He gave her permission to search his house and outbuildings. Police escorted her to the neighbor's house. She knew where the key was and opened the back door. The police said they would wait outside. With trepidation she entered the house, called out to silence, thoroughly searched the downstairs, and found no one or anything out of place. She went upstairs and thought about someone who could jump out at her. No one was upstairs and nothing was out of place. Searching in the barn would be a challenge. It was full of tractors and equipment blocking a direct line of sight. There was no one in the barn. There was no immediate danger so the police left saying they would return tomorrow.

The Slate family and barn clients were all asking the same question "Why Viking Hill Farm?" From the main road the driveway appears to end at the house. How did this person know the driveway ended at the edge of the swamp and a black SUV would be invisible in the thick overgrowth. Checking GPS, it showed the driveway going to the back of the property. Everyone tried to remember if they saw a black SUV at the barn. We were all on alert and took notice of our surroundings. The family felt violated. Their property of tranquility had an uninvited intruder.

That afternoon there was a frantic search for keys to lock and secure the buildings. This became an arduous task since the keys to all the buildings were in a pile in a drawer, unlabeled. Barns do not get locked as a safety feature if the horses had to exit quickly. The barn manager lived in the apartment above the barn since someone must always be in the barn. She knew her family was concerned about her being alone, but she had more alarm systems than any of us.

Her dogs knew the difference between night creature noises, horse sounds and a person moving around; they would bark if it was a person. At night, the barn doors are closed to keep the night creatures out of the barn. The doors are heavy wood and are pulled together to close them. They have metal rollers that ride on a metal track. The noise pulling them open would wake the manager, the dogs, and the horses.

The State Police came back the next day. They stopped at the office by the house where Leah and I worked. They introduced themselves and showed their identification. They came into the office and sat at the conference room table with Leah. They laid a transparent plastic evidence bag on the table; the items they retrieved from the car. I sat at my desk and listened.

The Victoria's Secret bag had women's underwear inside. The items on the passenger seat were a passport, driver's license, divorce papers, the title to the car and a phone. I thought who would put all their important papers and identification in the car then abandon it? This was more than a person ditching the car and walking away.

The owner of the car was Michael Sivick who lived in Monroe,

New York. He was no stranger to the police as they had confrontations with him before. He was a cross dresser and frequented the gay bar in Goshen. The last time anyone saw him was at the bar Saturday, March 16th dressed in women's clothing. That was the first night I was staying at the house when the dogs started barking at 1:13 a.m. on March 17th. Leah looked in my direction and I knew she did not want me to say anything about that night. The police questioned Leah if she knew Sivick or had done business with him. Her answer was no.

After the initial investigation of the area where the car was found, the police asked if they could use a helicopter to look at the area from above. During the day, the horses are in the paddocks and low flying aircraft could spook them. She gave them an ok and asked if they could fly as high as possible. If they needed to use the helicopter another day, they would let her know. In a helicopter the police could see a wide area of the swamp, trees, and farm fields. The canopy of the trees was thick and looking up from the ground did not give a clear view to the top. They would be able to see if Martin were hanging in a tree. The helicopter was there the next day and searched for a long time. The police found nothing.

For the next two weeks the police detectives were there every day expanding the search area, taking pictures and measurements and still no new evidence. While the detectives searched the farm, another detective was asking questions at the bar in Goshen. They also talked with Martin's neighbors in Monroe. They decided to bring in a search dog to sniff the area and asked Leah if it would be ok. It would be ok if the dog were on a leash and not running around. The next day they arrived with a German Shepard. They spent a long time searching, but the dog did not have any hits. Where was this man?

Leah suggested the police hire the Amigo Search and Rescue Dogs located in Goshen. Their dogs were trained to sniff for cadavers. Two days later, two black SUV's parked by the office. We both went outside, and Leah told them the story and why we needed a cadaver dog. I walked over to the SUV with the dog. I was impressed with the size and confirmation of the German Shephard. Leah would drive to the location where the dog was to search. When the Amigo team came to the car to follow Leah, the dog barked loudly. They said, "he is ready to go to work." It was hours before they returned to the office. We were both hoping the dog would find evidence of a person and put an end to this mystery. Their news was disappointing. The dog had one hit; it was an animal carcass.

The last place to look was the sinister Purgatory Swamp. The next time the police came back they brought two divers to search the bottom of the swamp. Just thinking about going in the water of the swamp gave me the "heebie jeebies." The water was deep brown covered with decaying vegetation, and a putrid smell. The diver's search lasted 10 minutes. Their activity stirred up the silt from the bottom reducing visibility to a cloudy two feet. They found nothing for the time they were in the water.

We all had an opinion about the hidden SUV. For some unknown reason Martin had to get rid of the car, so he drove it to the back of the property. Another car followed and they both left the farm by the driveway to the main road. Or he walked across the farm fields to Coleman Road where a car was waiting for him. Either suggestion would work but why did he leave all his identification in the car? How could he travel anywhere without identification? The police could not find this man in the local area, and they had no physical evidence of him being on the farm or at the neighbor's property. Was this man's disappearance intentional?

For days there was a police presence on the property. This was a high priority case since crimes like this did not happen in Goshen. When the police arrived, they always stopped at the office to show their badges and give us their names. They asked permission to go down and look at the scene again. It made me laugh at the way the detectives were dressed. They had on suits wearing muck boots. The police did a search on Martin's phone and got a location ping at the top of the driveway at the farm. This was early Sunday morning on March 17th. I struck out; three chances I had to prevent this mystery from happening. If I had just looked out the window.

The police kept the phone. After they made an inventory of the other items found in the car, they gave Leah the envelope. We were anxious to look at them. The divorce papers showed his divorce from his wife was recent. His driver's license picture showed a gruff person. The passport was interesting. A few pages were empty but the stamps on the rest of the pages were Bolivia, Columbia, and Brazil. All three of these countries ship illegal drugs to the United States and Martin could be involved in smuggling drugs. We both had the feeling he had to disappear because the drug cartel was after him.

The abandonment of the car became a great concern for all of us. Every day our anxiety increased when the police did not find any more clues. Could the drug cartel have been on the property and drove the car to the swamp? From now on, Leah instructed me to look out the office window and identify every car and truck that came in the driveway. If I did not recognize the vehicle, I was to phone her.

Occasionally, I was in the office by myself and now I kept the door locked. I made the decision to leave the office by dusk. Until the police arrested Martin, I felt uneasy.

Both of us were curious who Martin Sivick was. Leah did a search on Facebook, and his page came up. He lived in Monroe, NY. There was a picture of Martin, his wife and their five children. Leah found a phone number for the residence. Both of us asked the question at the same time. "Should we call it." Leach dialed the number; it rang several times before it was answered.

A woman's soft voice said, "hello." Leah introduced herself and asked for Martin, her husband. There was silence. Then she asked if this was Mrs. Janet Sivick. Her reply was yes. Leah told her about the abandoned car on her property and the important documents that were found inside. Janet wanted to tell her story but was guarded about the information she gave us. Both of us noticed she did not ask any questions about her husband.

Janet, with her five children, moved to California after filing for divorce. She was afraid of Martin and feared for the safety of her children. His behavior was bizarre with violent episodes of anger, yelling and breaking furniture. He was abusive to her, stole her underwear and wore women's clothing. He recently lost his job, withdrew all the money from their bank accounts, and maxed out the credit cards.

Leah summarized the event of the last two weeks of the abandoned car at the edge of the swamp, and the searches by the police that had no results. The only question Janet asked, "was there a key with the car?" No one saw a key and the police did not have one in the evidence bag. Janet said her babysitter was living in the house in Monroe and she would have a spare key. The police picked up the spare car key and kept it until they released the car. Janet requested the papers from the car be mailed to her in California. The passport, divorce papers and title were mailed "next day delivery." She called the next day to say she received the information.

Shortly after the phone call to Janet, the police gave the Slates permission to remove the car from the muck. A farm tractor pulled the car from the muck onto the driveway. Her daughter put the key in the ignition and after two tries, the car started. Slowly the car was driven to the back of the barn to wash the mud off. Riders in the barn gathered to look at the abandoned car. They felt as if they were part of the story.

Once the car was clean, it was parked by the office. It was backed up to a stone wall with heavy equipment in front of it and the doors locked. If Martin came back for the car, he would not be able to drive it off the property. No one was comfortable with the car parked that close to the house or office. I was concerned because it was parked in front of the office window where my desk was. To be safe the car was moved to an undisclosed location.

Before moving the car to another location, Leah did a thorough search of the car and found a loaded .45 pistol and a black bag with ammunition under the front seat. The gun was given to the police. More questions arose. Why did Martin have a loaded gun in the car? Was he going to use it on himself or someone else? Who was he running from that he needed a loaded gun? This was no longer about an abandoned car; it was a crime. A crime scene among the farm fields.

Leah called Janet to tell her she had the key to the car and suggested it be shipped to California by car transport. Janet said she could not afford to have it shipped. The car would stay at the farm until other arrangements were made. Several days later Janet called and said her father, who lived in the area, would drive the car to California. Leah had a mechanic check that the car was mechanically sound and then to the car wash for cleaning. It was a newer car and in good condition. Janet's father came for the car, and it was finally on its way to California. Was this the end to the mystery? No.

The car was a topic of discussion in the barn for a long time. The barn workers taking care of the horses rarely stopped to listen to conversations but one of the workers overheard a conservation and put two and two together. A year ago, Jason, a barn worker who lived in Monroe, would often talk about his neighbor Martin Sivick. He was fascinated by his hobby of rebuilding firearms in his basement. Jason talked about his diverse collection.

On numerous occasions Jason had driven the manure wagon down the dirt road to the back of the property to empty the wagon. Finally, we knew why that secluded spot was selected to abandon a car. The barn worker gave the information to Leah who called the police with the latest information. The police went to Jason's house to interview him. He pled the fifth. The police had no reason to arrest him, although he participated in the crime. What was the connection between Jason and Martin? He would be on the police radar.

Leah believed this to be a serious situation. Martin had to be a criminal on the run. The unknown places in his passport, the gun under the front seat, rebuilding guns in his basement, and no one had seen him since March 16th. All this information suggested his participation in illegal activities. This man was not just missing but permanently missing.

Janet's story was a little vague. She gave us details of her husband that we already knew.

She lived with this man and had to know all the places he traveled to and his hobby of rebuilding guns in his basement. Why did the babysitter live in the house? Leah and I felt confident that she knew of her husband's dealings and why he disappeared. Either she was running away or part of the crime.

We both believed that the disappearance of Martin Sivick was a Mafia hit. It was their classical "modus operandi" of getting rid of people permanently who crossed them. Martin was at the bar in Goshen on March 16th. When the dogs started barking on March 17th at 1:13 a.m. Martin was already dead. The car was abandoned at Viking Hill Farm by Purgatory Swamp thinking it would rot away. The Mafia never anticipated that the car would be found.

It has been several years since these events happened in 2022. The State Police detectives occasionally stop by to update the Slates of any progress on the case. There is no additional news. They are keeping the case open as a missing person's case. The case will remain open until Martin Sivick is found dead or alive.

The Slates added additional security to the property to make everyone a little more at ease. This will be the story of Viking Hill Farm forever.

Underground Railroad
1700's – 1865

The Underground Railroad referred to a network of trails, roads, rivers and railroads that were used by slaves escaping the South. It was their roadmap to freedom. They traveled at night to escape the slave owners hired men who were instructed to capture and return them to the slave camps.

Abolitionists, Quakers and free African Americans aided the slaves in their journey to freedom. There was a network of safe houses where slaves could find food, shelter, and medical care. The safe houses had to operate without drawing the attention of the law.

Shelter was a hidden space in barns, houses, tunnels, and false spaces under the floor. Traveling by wagon, the slaves were hidden among the cargo, sometimes in barrels, crates and false areas under the wagon.

Slaves travelled through the eastern states of New Jersey, Pennsylvania, and New York. Some stayed in Philadelphia others were headed to Canada. For some their destination was Goshen, New

York and the Erie railroad. Goshen had several safe houses where slaves waited to take the "milk train" to Newburgh. Guides would be waiting in Newburgh to take them farther to the North. The Erie railroad expanded in 1851 providing a direct line from Newburgh to Buffalo, New York. Many slaves traveled to Buffalo, New York by the Erie Railroad.

One of Goshen's staunch supporters, Hon. Ambrose S. Murray of Goshen was against slavery. He was director of the railroad, bank president and a representative in Congress. By his generosity he supplied special tickets for slaves to travel on the Erie railroad.

It is estimated that 100,000 slaves escaped by the Underground Railroad.

Anna Elizabeth Dickinson

1842 – 1932

"AMERICA'S CIVIL WAR JOAN OF ARC"

ANNA ELIZABETH DICKINSON
1842 - 1932
"AMERICA'S CIVIL WAR JOAN OF ARC"

In January of 1864, President Lincoln invited Anna to address Congress, the Cabinet and the Supreme Court, to rally support for the Union cause and the fight against slavery.

Anna devoted the rest of her life to justice, liberty and basic human rights for all people: male or female, black or white, rich or poor; and contributed to the 15th Amendment, prohibiting the disenfranchisement of any person based on race, sex, color or previous servitude.

Anna Dickinson lived at this site, in the Village of Goshen, for the last forty-one years of her life.

"My head and heart, soul and brain, were all on fire with the words I must speak"

22 West Main Street, Goshen, New York

Inscription on Plaque

In January 1864, President Lincoln invited Anna Elizabeth Dickinson to address Congress, the

Cabinet, and the Supreme Court, to rally support for the Union cause and the fight against slavery.

Anna devoted the rest of her life to justice, liberty, and basic human rights for all people: male or female, black or white, rich or poor, and contributed to the 15th Amendment, prohibiting the disenfranchisement of any person based on race, sex, color, or previous servitude.

Anna Dickinson lived at this site, in the Village of Goshen, for the last forty-one years of her life.

"My head and heart, soul and brain, were all on fire with the words I must speak"

Anna Elizabeth Dickinson was born on October 28, 1842, in Philadelphia, Pennsylvania. Her parents John and Mary Edmundson were Quakers and abolitionists. She was the youngest of three brothers and one sister. Her education was at the Friends Select School of Philadelphia and at the Westtown School in West Chester. In 1857, at the age of 15, she went to work as a copyist, a teacher in Berks County, Pennsylvania, and as a clerk for the United States Mint.

Her life was devoted to women's rights, abolition of slavery, African American rights, and temperance. Her reputation as a civil rights speaker became her life, and her speaking schedule at times was every other night. Her first major speech, February 27, 1861, in Philadelphia, Pennsylvania, was a two-hour speech on *The Rights and Wrongs of Women*. In 1863, Dickinson toured the country giving speeches on behalf of the Republican Party.

After the Civil War ended in 1865, audiences wanted to be entertained rather than lectured about serious topics. In 1872 Dickinson campaigned for Horace Greeley, a Democratic presidential candidate; causing her lecturing career to decline. Her speech in 1888 for the Republican candidate for President ended her lecturing career. Dickinson called Grover Cleveland the "hangman of Buffalo" and waved a bloody shirt.

With her speaking career over, Ralph Meeker invited Dickinson to come to Colorado to experience the wonders of his state. Dickinson climbed Pikes Peak, Mount Lincoln, Grays Peak, and Mount Elbert in three weeks. Their climb required the use of mules or horses, and Dickson wore trousers. The newspaper, Boulder County News, reported Dickinson wore trousers and the public was aghast. Dickinson had hoped that the papers covering her ascents of the peaks would revive her speaking career.

After Dickinson had a disastrous end to her speaking career, she tried authoring books and acting. Neither adventure resulted in success. Dickinson was head of the household and primary wage-earner for her mother, sister, and a servant. She moved to West Pittston, Pennsylvania in 1883 to live with her sister and 95-year-old mother. Her mother Mary died in 1889.

Two years after her mother's death, Dickinson exhibited signs of paranoia. In February 1891, her sister Susan committed her to Danville State Hospital for the Insane. At Anna's insistence, she was transferred to Interpines Sanitarium in Goshen, New York. Dr. Seward of Interpines and her friends sued the newspapers for printing false information that she was insane. She won the case but lost her supporters and friends because of her antagonistic behavior. Dickinson died in 1932 of cerebral apoplexy.

The World War II Liberty Ship, SS Anna Dickinson, was named in her honor for being the first woman to address the U.S. Congress. The ship was launched September 4, 1944. It was decommissioned on September 8, 1949. It was sold for scrap on March 4, 1961.

Church Park Historic District

CHURCH PARK HISTORIC DISTRICT HAS BEEN PLACED ON THE NATIONAL REGISTER OF HISTORIC PLACES IN 1980 BY THE UNITED STATES DEPARTMENT OF INTERIOR

WILLIAM C. POMEROY FOUNDATION 2018   146

Main Street, Park Place and South Church Road

The church park historic district is a triangular shaped piece of property within the boundaries of Main Street, Park Place and South Church Street. There are two historical buildings on the property. The First Presbyterian Church and the 1773 courthouse. The Presbyterian Church was the first church in Orange County. The 1773 courthouse building was repurposed as the county office building in 1887.

The church was established in 1724. A wooden church building was completed in 1810, and a stone church building was dedicated on November 22, 1871. The church building is blue limestone, and the 186-foot-tall spire is solid stone. The spire towers above the landscape and can be seen from a long distance. It is the subject of many photographers and is the pride of Goshen.

The large beautiful grassy area with shade trees and benches in front of the church is referred to as the Church Park. Every year many community activities are held here. The town's business was conducted here for two reasons. It was in the center of town and the large area could accommodate many people. It has the past reputation of having the large Cottonwood hanging tree where Claudius Smith and others were "hanged until dead."

Claudius Smith

COWBOY OF THE RAMAPOS

1736 – 1779

LEGENDS & LORE
CLAUDIUS SMITH
REPUTED TORY MARAUDER
HANGED NEARBY IN 1779.
HIS SKULL BELIEVED EMBEDDED
IN MASONRY OVER FRONT DOOR
OF THIS 1841 COURTHOUSE.
NEW YORK FOLKLORE SOCIETY
WILLIAM C. POMEROY FOUNDATION 2016   22

101 Main Street

Claudius Smith was born in Brookhaven, New York in 1736. He moved with his family to Orange County, New York in 1741. Smith, as an adult, was known as the American Revolutionist Tory Marauder. He earned the title, "Cowboy of the Ramapos" by using guerrilla tactics against Patriot civilians.

Smith's gang included his two sons, Richard and James, James Flewelling, Lieutenant James Moody, and Indian Chief Joseph Brant of the Butler's Rangers. He was known as "Robin Hood" for robbing travelers on the Orange Turnpike and giving the money to the poor. He and his gang targeted wealthy Patriots stealing horses, cattle, silverware, and other valuable items.

On one of their raids, they murdered Patriot Major Nathaniel Strong. Governor George Clinton issued a warrant for Smith's arrest and a $1,200 reward for his capture. The gang evaded capture by hiding in their network of caves. Orange County has memorialized one of his caves, "Claudius Smiths Den" located in Orange County's Harriman State Park.

After a reward was posted for his capture by Governor Clinton, Smith retreated to a friend's house in Smithtown, Long Island. He knew the area of Long Island since the house where he was born was in Brookhaven, Long Island. Major Jesse Brush discovered he was at his friend's house on Long Island, formed a pose from Connecticut, and stormed the friend's house capturing Smith. The Tory Marauder was taken to Goshen.

Smith was taken to the 1727 courthouse and put in jail. The jail was in the basement. On January 13, 1779, the courts charged him with three counts of robbery and ordered his death by hanging. His execution date was scheduled for January 29, 1779.

Smith's mother Meriam, had warned Claudius unless he reformed, he would "die with his boots on." Before hanging from the famous Cottonwood tree in Church Park, he removed his boots. Three other people also died by hanging that day. Smiths' son James, Thomas Detmar, and James Gordon.

Legend has it that Smith's skull was filled with mortar and placed in the edifice of the 1841 Court House.

Erie Station
1841 – 1983

1 Grand Avenue

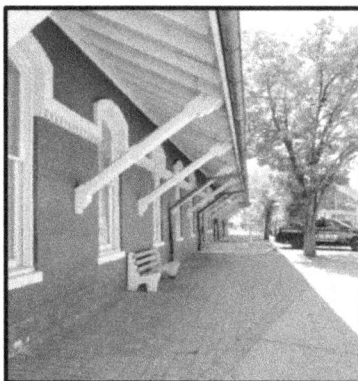
Goshen Village Police Station

The first train cars of the New York and Erie Railroad arrived in Goshen on September 23, 1841. The town had a day of celebration. The train was pulled by Locomotive No.4 named "Orange" to honor Orange County, New York. As train travel increased the small Goshen station was overwhelmed with passengers and needed to be replaced. In 1867 a new Erie Depot Station was built.

In May 1851, Daniel Webster, New York Secretary of State, was aboard the first nonstop train from Piermont-on-Hudson to Dunkirk, New York. It was the inaugural trip celebrating the completion of the New York & Erie Railroad as the longest railroad in the United States at the time.

In 1983 Orange County approved the Metro North Railroad, the Graham Line, as the primary train to service the North. The

Erie line in Goshen was abandoned; the rails were ripped up in 1984. The Erie line was in service for 140 years.

The Erie train station building was repurposed as the Goshen Village Police Station in 1986. "Depot" was removed from the name since it was no longer an active train station.

General Ulysses S. Grant

APRIL 27, 1822 – JULY 23, 1885

PRESIDENT ULYSSES S. GRANT 1869 – 1877

210 West Main Street

General Ulysses S. Grant visited Goshen frequently, staying at Stonyford farm with friends. On occasion he would attend the harness races at the Goshen track.

On his way to the Erie train station, he would stop to visit his friend Gen. John A. Rawlings, who lived on Main Street. John Rawlings was Grants Chief of Staff in the American Civil War.

Rawlings lived in the house with his three children and their grandmother, Sarah Smith. Grant enjoyed playing with Rawlings three children, Mary, Willie and Violet. The children adored Grant and looked forward to his visits.

John Rawlings died September 6, 1869. He was 38 years old. Rawlings will appointed Grant the care of his three children known as "wards." Grant would be responsible for the care and upbringing of the Rawlings children.

Goshen Courts
1727 –PRESENT

The first New York assembly was held on October 17, 1683, when the Province of New York was divided into twelve counties. The court of General Sessions, initially known as the Court of Quarter Sessions, had civil and criminal jurisdiction. Goshen became the center for county government.

In 1727 Goshen was designated as a half-shire town of Orange County. It served as one of two county seats created by establishing counties. The county court of Goshen shared duties with Newburgh for 172 years, until 1970 when Orange County received a new charter.

The first courthouse and jail in Goshen was built in 1727 on the site where the Orange Inn would be built. The old courthouse was demolished in 1776.

A new courthouse was built in 1773, across the street, from the original courthouse. It was a plain two-story building. The sheriff's office and living quarters were on the first floor, the court rooms were on the second floor, and a jail was built in the basement.

1773 Courthouse, 255 Main Street

1841 Courthouse
101 Main Street, Goshen

1967, Paul Randolph Brutalist Style
Building, Goshen, New York

The county clerk's office was moved from the courthouse to this building in 1851. The building's purpose changed in 1887 when it became the Orange County Administration Offices. The mansard roof was removed in 1937 to add a third floor.

The building is located behind the Presbyterian Church and still in use today.

Two new courthouses, one in Goshen and one in Newburgh, were built in April 1841. Both were built in the Greek Revival style. Thorton M. Niven was the architect.

The first Orange County Fair was held in Goshen at the courthouse on November 17, 1841. The one-day event attracted farmers from across the county to view exhibits of cattle, horses and vegetables.

The 1841 Courthouse was used for 130 years.

In 1970, the half-shire Newburgh courthouse was closed making Goshen the County Seat. A new Orange County Government Center building was needed. Building a new courthouse was a nine-year debate by the county Board of Supervisors.

Architect Paul Randolph designed the brutalist style new Orange County Government Center building.

The residents in town had an opinion about the style of the Paul Randolph Brutalist style building. Some said it was beautiful; some said it was ugly and did not represent the historical character of the town.

After several years of poor maintenance, the building was falling apart. The town discussed the cost of demolition and construction of a new building versus the cost of restoration. Restoration was the choice. The vote was 11 to 10.

A new, larger Orange County building for the activities of the courts, was built in 1998 behind the Paul Randolph building. The new building is glass and glimmer.

A new 90-million-dollar jail opened in 2000, located at 110 Wells Farm Road, Goshen, New York.

1998
Glass and Steel Government building
255 Main Street, Goshen, NY

Goshen Emergency Hospital
1908 – 1915

GOSHEN EMERGENCY HOSPITAL ESTABLISHED HERE, 1908, BY SUSAN R. BACON, PROVIDED 3 BEDS, 1 COT. STAFFED BY NURSE MARY BYRNE & DOCTORS CONDICT, DENNIS, HAMILTON, AND McGEOCH. (918-00009I)

136 West Street

Goshen had several doctors in town to treat those who got sick or needed a stitch or two. Goshen needed an emergency hospital for serious injuries, especially those that happened around the railroad. Many times, the newspaper had headlines, "Man hurt on railroad."

Mrs. Susan Randall Bacon, wife of Congressman Henry Bacon, organized a meeting at the home of Miss Alma E. Merriam inviting other local women to discuss her idea of establishing an emergency hospital in the village. It would be a daunting task since they had no medical experience or how to run a hospital.

That meeting was held on May 8, 1908, where Mrs. Bacon presented plans and papers of incorporation. Two months later a four-room upstairs apartment in the Tuthill building at 136 West Street was rented. Two of the rooms would be for patients and nurse Miss Mary Byrne. Four doctors would be the staff for the hospital. The hospital opened on July 4, 1908.

Miss Mary Byrne lived at the hospital since she was the only person to take care of the patients. Occasionally, her sister Theresa would relieve her of her duties to do errands or attend church. In 1910 the Board approved two initiatives. Admission cards would be given to the Goshen doctors to fill out, relieving Miss Byrne from having to make admission decisions. A boy was hired to carry fresh water upstairs in the morning and evening. He would also remove the trash and old dressings.

The emergency hospital was an asset to the town. The injured patient would be stabilized and either sent home, to the care of their doctor, or to a hospital in another town. In 1915 they received a donation from Luella M. VanLeuven of her large house to open the Goshen Hospital.

The brick Tuthill building still stands at 136 West Street.

Goshen Hospital
1915 – 1967

225 Greenwich Avenue

In 1915 The Goshen Emergency Hospital received a donation from Luella Morris VanLeuven of her house for a hospital. The house was a large mansard roof residence with seven large columns across the front entrance. Buildings were added for the nurses' quarters and a maternity wing

In 1922, Gates Wallace McGarrah, Executive Chairman of Chase National Bank of New York City, and his wife Elizabeth paid for a new maternity ward. Medical instruments were donated by the widow of Dr. Daniel Condict. Donovan Funeral Home provided ambulances. In 1955, Susan R. Bacon obtained a $25,000 donation from the Ford Foundation.

The town rallied around the new hospital with donations of money, supplies, equipment, and time. There were many fund-raising events. Board members rolled up their sleeves to help the nurses, attended to patients, and cook meals.

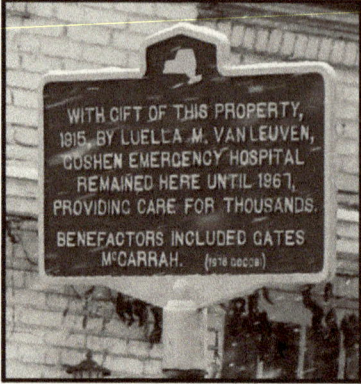

WITH GIFT OF THIS PROPERTY,
1915, BY LUELLA M. VAN LEUVEN,
GOSHEN EMERGENCY HOSPITAL
REMAINED HERE UNTIL 1967,
PROVIDING CARE FOR THOUSANDS.

BENEFACTORS INCLUDED GATES
McCARRAH.

Transfer of Property

Susan R. Bacon, who started the Goshen Emergency Hospital, died in 1955 after serving the hospital for 37 years.

A new hospital on Harriman Drive opened its doors in 1967, Arden Hill Hospital. Arden Hill Hospital was replaced by Orange Regional Hospital in Middletown, NY opening on August 5, 2011. On June 18, 2020, the name was changed to Garnet Health.

Goshen had a hospital for 103 years.

Goshen's Historic Track

44 Park Place, Goshen, New York

In 1790 a scrubland field along Greenwich Avenue, known as Fiddler's Green, would become Goshen's Historic Track. Early 19th century the area became a common meeting place for racing, training and breeding horses. Interest in Fiddler's Green declined around the 1820's and the area was forgotten.

The track was established in 1838 when the track was built around the circus grounds. Joseph Coates, a pioneer racetrack designer, bought the land in 1890. He refurbished the track and built a three-cornered track to train trotters. Coates named it the Goshen Mile track.

William H. Crane, a sports promoter and horse owner, bought the land in 1926. He named the track Good Time Park and began to hold racing events. One year later, it became a Grand Circuit track with large stables and a grandstand. The appointed track manager Rensselaer Weston named the track Goshen Historic Track in the

1900's. Over the years the shape of the track changed several times with structural improvements to the barns and property.

E. H. Harriman leased the track from Orange County Park Driving Association in the 1890's and gained stewardship of the track in 1909. He held the stewardship for 85 years before passing the responsibility of the track to Goshen Historic Track, Inc. in 1979.

In 1793, the thoroughbred Messenger, imported from England, was bought by Henry Astor of Long Island, New York. Messenger would be available for stud services at different farms in New York. In 1801, Anthony Dobbins of the Stagecoach Inn offered Messenger for stud service in his barn. Abadallah was sired in 1823 and his blood line sired Hambletonian (1849-1876), who became the sire of all Standardbreds. Because of Hambletonian's reputation, Goshen became known as the "Cradle of the Trotter." The Hambletonian race was held at the track from 1930-1956 before being moved to the Meadowlands, East Rutherford, New Jersey.

Horace Pippin

FEBRUARY 22, 1888 –JULY 6, 1946

AFRICAN AMERICAN FOLK ART PAINTER

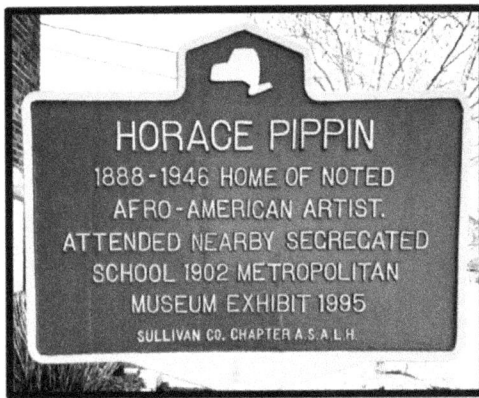

207 West Main Street

On February 22, 1888, Horace Pippin was born in West Chester, Pennsylvania, to Harriet Johnson Pippin. The family moved to Goshen, New York when Pippin was three years old. His mother was a domestic worker; his grandparents had been slaves. His mother Harriet raised him in a house located at 339 West Main Street. Today, it is a private residence.

The Civil War ended April 9,1865. Slavery was abolished but segregation was a way of life for the African American population. Segregation ended with the passage of the Civil Rights Act of 1964.

Pippin attended a colored school in Goshen and St. John's A.U.M.P. church (African United Methodist Protestant.)

Pippin was born to be an artist but had little opportunity to use his talent. His mother could not afford to buy him drawing materials.

St. John's A.U.M.P. Church
207 West Main Street, Goshen, NY

Horace Pippin
Self Portrait

He took every opportunity to express himself and would illustrate his spelling words. At the age of 10, he entered a drawing contest in a magazine and won a box of crayons and started coloring. After finishing sixth grade at the age of 14, his mother became ill. He left school to work and help his family. He worked mediocre jobs.

In 1917 he enlisted in the 15th regiment of the New York National Guard. He was assigned to the 369th infantry, an all-black unit that served in France. In combat he sustained an injury to his right shoulder, permanently disabling his right arm. He received an honorable discharge, and a disability pension. In 1920 he married Jennie Ora Fetherstone Wade Giles, and they moved to her home in West Chester, Pennsylvania.

Because of his disability, he could not obtain gainful employment and started to paint cigar boxes. He experimented with pyrography, burning imagery into wood panels. He discovered he could paint by supporting his weak working hand by holding it with his left hand. Horace Pippin started painting with oils in 1930.

For eight years, after moving to Pennsylvania, he painted with little recognition for his work. In 1937 N. C. Wyeth of Chester, Pennsylvania, spotted his work and eventually arranged for a one-person show of his work. The show resulted in his work being sold by a Philadelphia art dealer.

His paintings were exhibited in the Metropolitan Museum of Art and the Pennsylvania Academy of Fine Arts. Pippin had a successful exhibition at the Carlen Galleries in 1940 and was doing 15 paintings a year. Soon, his paintings were in demand, and he was considered the greatest Black painter of his time.

Pippins rise to fame, paralleled the folk-art revival of the 1930s. His work was called primitive, naïve, or innocent. The subjects for his paintings were inspired by African American genre scenes, portraits, and biblical scenes to politically charged historical scenes. His most famous historical painting was "John Brown Going to His Hanging."

The Goshen Public Library wrote to Horace Pippin asking him to exhibit his paintings at the library. He did not come to Goshen, instead, he painted "The Milkman of Goshen" shown at the Carnegie Institute Art Exhibition.

The Milkmen of Goshen
Horace Pippin, 1945

Pipin was not recognized as a painter until he was in his forties. His career as a famous painter was 15 years. His most important works were created at that time.

In 1946 Pippins wife Jeannie was committed to a mental hospital. A few weeks later Pippin died of a heart attack in his sleep. His wife Jeannie died two weeks later.

Maplewood
1816 –PRESENT

246 Main Street, Goshen, NY

Built in 1816, Maplewood was the home of Ambrose S. Murray and his family. His house was the location of the first Bank of Orange County, New York. Murray was dedicated and became the President of the bank in 1845. He served as Director of the Erie Railroad 1853-1867. In 1854 he was elected as a U.S. Representative in New York and was reelected in 1856.

Ambrose was a Wig and a strong opponent to slavery. He participated in their escape to the North. As director of the Erie Railroad, he obtained special marked train tickets for the escaped slaves to continue their journey to Canada.

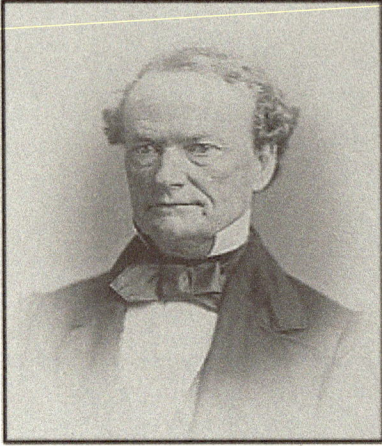

Ambrose Spencer Murray

During the American Civil War, he was on a committee to recruit and equip the troops of the Union Army. As Goshen's member of the Orange County Committee, he was to assemble the 124th New York Volunteer Infantry Regiment. Most of the recruits were from Orange County and the regiment was nicknamed the Orange Blossoms.

Ambrose Murray was born November 1807 and died November 1885. Ambrose and his wife Frances are buried in St. James cemetery in Goshen.

In 1976, Maplewood became the Goshen Village Hall.

Noah Webster

OCTOBER 16, 1758 –MAY 28, 1843

41 Webster Avenue

Noah Webster

An American lexicographer, testbook pioneer, English-language spelling reformer, political writer, editor, and author. He was known as the "Father of American Schlorship and Education.

Goshen Town Hall

Webster taught school for two years, 1782–1783 at the Farmer's Hall Academy located at 41 Webster Avenue, Goshen, New York. Today this is the Goshen Town Hall building. His historical marker is in an area off the main road that makes it difficult to spot.

Noah Webster was born in West Hartford, Connecticut

during the Colonial Era. His father was a farmer, deacon of the Congregational church, captain of the town's militia, and founder of the local book society. Today, that is the equivalent of our public library. Noah was home schooled by his mother with emphasis on spelling, mathemtics and music.

The local pastor schooled Noah in Latin and Greek to prepare him to enter Yale College. He graduated from Yale College in 1779. Under U. S. Supreme Court Justice Oliver Ellsworth he earned a law degree in 1781 but never practiced law.

While at Yale the American Revolutionary War broke out. He served in the Connecticut Militia, was a strong supporter of the American Revolution and the ratification of the Constitution. Webster founded the Connecticut Society for the Abolition of Slavery in 1791. At the time he was serving in the Connecticut House of Representatives.

He moved to New York City to edit the Federalist Party newspaper, and published the first daily newspaper, *"American Minerva."* In 1799 he wrote two massive books on the causes of "Epidemics and Pestilential Diseases." The medical profession gave him the title, "America's first epidemiologist."

It took Webester 50 plus or minus years to write the three volumes of the The Elementary Spelling Book. *The First Part of the Grammatical Institute of the English Language* was his first attempt to compile a spelling book for school children. The title was changed in 1786 to the *American Spelling Book.* The title was changed in 1829 to *The Elementary Spelling Book.*

The third edition of the speller, called the "Blue-Backed Speller," because of the blue cover, was used for the next one hundred years to teach children how to read, spell, and to pronounce words.

Webster published his first dictionary *"Compendious Dictionary of the English Language"* in 1828 at the age of 70. He wanted his work protected and advocated for the passage of the Copyright Act of 1831. At the age of 80, Webster was working on the second edition of his dictionary when he passed away in 1843. The rights to his dictionary were acquired from his estate by George and Charles Merriam. The dictionary we use today—Merriam Webster Dictionary.

Noah Webster was an intellectual visionary of the English language. He was ridiculed by many scholars but he persisted to accomplish his dreams. The above narrative is a snapshot of his accomplishments.

Old Stone Schoolhouse
1723 –1938
NY 17A 1.4 MILE SOUTH OF GOSHEN

In 1723, a local landowner deeded 20 acres to the community for a school. It was one of the first schools in Orange County and was in use for well over a century. Records show it was the oldest, active one-room schoolhouse in the United States.

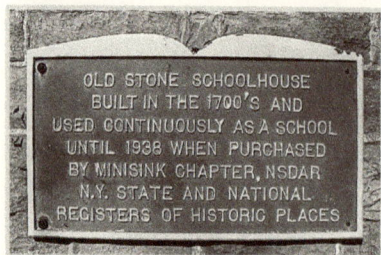

William Henry Seward, who lived in the village of Florida, walked three miles every day to attend the Old Stone Schoolhouse. Seward later became the United States Secretary of State. During the Revolutionary War, it is said General George Washington stopped at the school to talk with the children.

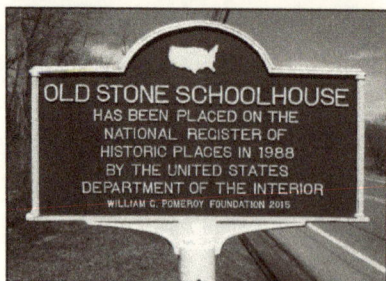

In later years, it was known as the Borden Quarry School because of an excavation site nearby. After the school closed in 1938, the Minisink Chapter, Daughters of the American Revolution (DAR) bought the property.

ABOUT THE AUTHOR

Life is like a thousand-piece puzzle. Find a piece and life continues. Sometimes, finding a piece that fits is elusive. Eventually, it's found.

I grew up in the country and became a 'country girl.' My interests were history, old things, nature and animals. Others could have the fast life of the cities, noise, crowds, and people frantically trying to get somewhere.

After getting married in 1971, we purchased a gentlemen's farm with an old stone farmhouse and barn in Worcester, Pennsylvania. It was falling apart, and I loved the challenge of restoring it. I went to Orphans Court in Philadelphia to find the original deed. The land was a grant from William Penn, soldiers from the American Revolution were buried on the property, and the house was dated 1786.

My daughter Amanda was born in 1979 and also embraced country life. We would sit on the back porch and enjoy our ice cream, eat watermelon and carve our Halloween pumpkins. She called the chickens cluck clucks and named our two pigs Runt and Grunt. She grew up with several dogs and many cats.

I sent her to an exclusive private school for her education. With her upbeat personality, she quickly made friends with everyone. Her classmates drove expensive cars, and Amanda drove a blue pick-up truck with a red fender. They all wanted to ride in her pick-up truck and would fill up the gas tank for the privilege.

After 26 years, I filed for divorce and left our restored farmhouse behind. I moved to Goshen, New York to be near my daughter and son-in-law. I fell in love with the historical town of Goshen.

www.ingramcontent.com/pod-product-compliance
Lightning Source LLC
Chambersburg PA
CBHW031139090426
42738CB00008B/1154